DiDA

D204
DIPLOMA IN DIGITAL APPLICATIONS
Book 4

Molly Wischhusen
Janet Snell
Jenny Johnson

Heinemann
Inspiring generations

Heinemann Educational Publishers
Halley Court, Jordan Hill, Oxford OX2 8EJ
Part of Harcourt Education

Heinemann is a registered trademark of
Harcourt Education Limited

Text © Molly Wischhusen, Janet Snell and Jenny Johnson, 2006

First published 2006

10 09 08 07 06
10 9 8 7 6 5 4 3 2 1

British Library Cataloguing in Publication Data is available
from the British Library on request.

10-digit ISBN 0 435 44985 0
13-digit ISBN 978 0 435449 85 8

Designed by Lorraine Inglis
Typeset by 🐦 Tek-Art, Croydon, Surrey
Printed by Bath Colourbooks Ltd
Cover photo: © Stock Image/Pixland/Alamy

Acknowledgements
Every effort has been made to contact copyright holders of material reproduced in
this book. Any omissions will be rectified in subsequent printings if notice is given
to the publishers.

Post-it® is a registered trademark of 3M.

Travelbug and *travelbug.co.uk* are fictitious names and have no connection with
any company with such names at the time of printing, or in the future.

Websites
Please note that the examples of websites suggested in this book were up to date at
the time of writing. It is essential for tutors to preview each site before using it to
ensure that the URL is still accurate and the content is appropriate. We suggest
tutors bookmark useful sites and consider enabling students to access them through
the school or college intranet.

Screen shots reprinted with permission from Microsoft Corporation.

Contents

Acknowledgements

A very special thank you to Samantha Moss and Jeanette Theaker students at Croydon College, who assisted in the preparation of the Graphics Unit by producing designs for the CD Player, the MP3 Player and the lollipops and patterns used as examples of cloning. We are full of admiration for their attitude to their work and wish them all the best for the future.

BAA plc
BBC
Department of Health
Department of Transport
Google
Haywards Heath College (now Central Sussex College)
Jade Teo
Lloyds TSB
Long Tall Sally
Royal Institute of Chartered Surveyors
Starfish Design and Print, Heathfield, East Sussex
Steve Holmes of Signet Construction Ltd, Eastbourne
VL Systems Ltd

Photo acknowledgements

The authors and publisher would like to thank the following for permission to reproduce photographs:

Canon Images – page 142
Getty Images/Photodisc – page 105
Rex Features – page 14
Sandisk – page 63

Dedications

I could not wish for better co-authors and friends to work with than Janet and Jenny. My very sincere appreciation to Janet for holding the fort for Jenny and me when we needed it. My thanks also to Elaine Tuffery and her colleagues for their understanding and support. As always the encouragement from my family and friends is invaluable and the arrival of Sophie Grace hardly delayed me at all!

Molly Wischhusen

My thanks to the team at Heinemann for their support and especially to my special friends Molly and Jenny, my husband Bob and all my family.

Janet Snell

I dedicate this book to my beloved husband Ray who died suddenly before it was completed.

My sincere thanks go to Molly and Janet and my sons Ian and Colin and my daughter-in-law Helen, without whose support I would not have been able to finish my contribution. Thanks also to the Heinemann team for their encouragement during what has been an extremely difficult time for me.

Jenny Johnson

Introduction

Welcome to the programme of study in digital applications. You may be studying for the Certificate or the Diploma in Digital Applications. These qualifications are designed to create confident users of digital applications, who are able to apply their skills purposefully and effectively.

Which units do you need to take?

- For the **Certificate** in Digital Applications (CiDA) you will achieve Unit 1 plus one other unit of your choosing.
- For the **Diploma** in Digital Applications (DiDA) you will achieve all four units.

Each unit is the equivalent of one GCSE. The assessment for each of the units is a summative project that is set by Edexcel, the awarding body.

This book provides you with the necessary knowledge and skills to complete Unit 4.

What do you have to do to succeed?

To enable you to complete the projects, you will need to use ICT efficiently, legally and safely. You will learn all about this in Part 2, Section 1 on standard ways of working.

You will also need to develop ICT skills in a wide variety of software applications, which you then apply to complete the projects. ICT skills are developed in Part 2, Section 2: see the Skills Checklist on pages 4–9.

✔ TiP

In preparing for your project it is essential for you to build up expertise in each of the software packages that you will be using. The project will consist of a number of tasks, each of which will require careful planning and thoughtful implementation. Therefore it is vital that you work steadily, allowing plenty of time for each task. You will find some tasks cannot be completed unless you have finished others.

In addition, you must

- learn how to plan, review and evaluate your projects
- learn what is meant by an e-portfolio and create one
- understand the topics specific to this unit.

The aim of Unit 4 is to give you hands-on experience of how ICT can improve the efficiency and competitiveness of enterprises. Every product you produce must be fit for its intended purpose. Each of the separate activities will be given a range of possible marks. The quality and complexity of your work will determine the mark you receive for each activity.

The completed project will **not** be printed out in the traditional way. Instead you will create an **e-portfolio** that displays your work in electronic form. An e-portfolio is rather like a website where links lead the user to the different activities you have been asked to complete. The e-portfolio will be assessed by an internal assessor and an external moderator.

Features of the book

Many of the illustrations and activities in the book are centred around a fictitious company called Travelbug. Throughout the book you will find hints, tips and tasks to help you develop the skills, knowledge and understanding you need to successfully achieve your qualification.

Skills evidence – a general signpost to advise you when to save results in activities undertaken in the skills chapters, for possible inclusion in your e-portfolio

Go out and try! – practice tasks to help you develop the skills that have been described in that section of the book

Jargon buster – explanations of some of the technical language which may be unfamiliar

Skills check – cross-references to related information in other parts of the book

Think it over – activities to get you thinking about how you will go about or prepare for the practical tasks

Tip – guidance, notes and hints to help you

Skills builder task – practice closely linked to the skills you will need to complete your summative projects (not as demanding as the full project required by Edexcel, but it will be good preparation for learning how to develop an e-portfolio)

Assessment hint – hints to guide you on what would make the difference to achieving a merit, credit or distinction compared to a pass grade

Much of the knowledge and many of the skills required for DiDA Unit 1 are also required for Unit 4. These are provided again in this book to ensure you have all the necessary information for Unit 4 to refer to in one book. A blue tab down the edge of the page denotes knowledge and skills that you should have covered in Unit 1. Knowledge and skills that were not covered in Unit 1 have no blue tab down the edge of the page.

We wish you good luck and hope you enjoy your course.

Molly Wischhusen
Janet Snell
Jenny Johnson

PART 1

Unit 4 ICT in Enterprise

Introduction

Every year, hundreds of people start a new business. Their ideas stem from new inventions, turning hobbies into a business, providing a service, and so on. If you had a brilliant idea for a new business, people would think you were very enterprising. They would admire you for taking the risk of setting up a new business enterprise and developing a business opportunity.

Because any such venture carries a risk, it essential that you carry out careful planning and preparation to make sure the idea is viable. For example, you would need to

- carry out market research to make sure there is sufficient interest
- produce financial forecasts
- develop a business plan
- develop a corporate identity
- present your plans to people whose support you need – the bank manager, for example
- promote your business.

LEARNING OUTCOMES

After working through this chapter you should be able to

✓ use ICT effectively to help you research and plan for the launch of a new business enterprise.

How will I be assessed?

You will be given a project brief for this unit and you will be required to use ICT to explore and plan for a business activity. The project brief will specify exactly what you will be required to produce. You can expect to spend about 30 hours working on the assessment for this unit. You will be assessed on **six** separate activities as follows:

1 Plan and manage the project
2 Investigate an enterprise opportunity

3 Create a corporate image
4 Promote a product or service
5 Use an e-portfolio to present an enterprise proposal
6 Carry out an end-of-project review.

The marks you will be awarded will depend on the quality and complexity of your work and your teacher will be able to show you how the marks are allocated against each activity.

The project brief will give you hints and tips on successfully completing the assessment. The skills chapters provide help on the various software applications you can choose to use. In addition, you will find detailed guidance throughout this chapter, and we strongly suggest you also read the following chapters, which contain specific help on completing the assessments:

- Standard ways of working
- Project planning
- Review and evaluation
- Creating an e-portfolio.

Skills file

The table below lists all the skills required to complete this unit successfully. The pages where you will find these skills explained are identified in the Page column. You should have already covered those which have a blue tab in Unit 1.

ARTWORK AND IMAGING SOFTWARE

	Page
select and capture images:	
• use a digital camera	142
• use a scanner	142
• download images from the Internet	156
• use clip art and library images	141
modify images:	
• group and ungroup	143
• cut, paste, crop, trim, resize	144
• align, rotate	145
choose appropriate image resolutions and file formats for	
• print publications	147
• digital publications	147

COLLABORATIVE SOFTWARE

EMAIL

INTERNET AND INTRANETS

SPREADSHEET SOFTWARE

WEB AUTHORING SOFTWARE

WORD-PROCESSING SOFTWARE

Identifying a business opportunity

If identifying a business opportunity were an easy process, we would all be running our own successful businesses! Unfortunately, it is not easy and requires a lot of careful planning, quite apart from having the idea in the first place. Businesses that are successful have usually discovered a gap in the market and stepped in to fill that niche before anyone else. The growth of the Internet in recent years has provided new avenues for existing business such as banking and retail, and opened up new business ventures such as eBay and lastminute.com. The owners of these businesses were fortunate to have had the ideas and to have discovered the gap in the market.

A business idea might be

- developing a new product or service that you feel would be useful
- marketing a new invention
- expanding an existing business into a new line of work
- turning a hobby into a business
- developing an idea that you have seen somewhere else.

Developing an idea for a business is a creative process, and one that can't be rushed. Brainstorming is one way to generate ideas, and you have probably been doing this throughout the planning of your other projects. You will have drawn up mind maps to help you record and organise your ideas. In the Project Planning Software chapter (page 199) we look at specialist mind-mapping software that you can use to help you plan and organise your ideas. You will be using software such as this to develop your project.

Once an idea has taken shape, you must look at the viability of your new business venture and carry out some detailed market research. Market research is a fact-finding exercise carried out by a business to identify product development opportunities. In carrying out this research, businesses will gather information about the goods and services their customers want, to enable them to supply those products. When contemplating the launch of a new product or service, a business would want to find answers to the following questions:

- Is there a demand for the product/service?
- What is the customer profile?
- What area will the customers be from?
- How much are they prepared to pay?
- What level of quality/service do they require?
- What competition is there?
- When and how can you sell your product/service?
- how will the business be affected by changing trends and fashions?
- What materials and supplies will you need and where can you find them?

Let's look at each of these in turn.

Demand

If you are starting on a new venture, you will be very excited about your business idea and could easily get carried away with it. However, it is essential you ensure that there is a demand for your product or service and that prospective customers are as enthusiastic as you are. You must make sure that your product or service is different from anything else in the local market and that customers will be prepared to pay for it. If you are offering a product similar to that of another local business, you must be sure that the market is big enough for both of you. If you are producing something new,

Jargon buster

People who buy **products** from a business are called **customers**; those who pay for **services** are called **clients**.

you might consider 'testing' the market to find out how people react to the product or service before you spend too much time pursuing your idea. If you are thinking of turning an interest or hobby into a business, make sure that there are potential customers who might want to share your interest.

Customer profile

Customers are the key to any successful business. The more you know about your potential customers, the better the chances of success. Customers don't just appear when you open your doors for the first time; you must make sure your business attracts them in. If you are thinking of opening a business in a shopping area, one way to find out who your potential customers are likely to be is to observe and count them. There would be little point in opening a shop selling trendy fashion items if the local market comprised mainly senior citizens. If you have a new service in mind, you must make sure that there are enough people in the area who would use the service. For example, in a community where a large proportion of families are on low incomes, a cleaning or ironing service would probably not be within their means.

Customer location

You will need to consider if your product or service can rely on the local market alone or whether it must attract customers from a wider area. For example, a corner shop would generally expect to attract customers from the surrounding roads, and would probably serve a large number of regular customers. A clothes shop in the high street of a larger town would expect their customers to come from a wider area, and the shop would probably pick up a considerable amount of passing trade. If you were pursuing the cleaning or ironing service, would you have to spend time travelling to your clients? If this was the case, you might waste a lot of time earning nothing because you were travelling and not cleaning.

Price

Your customers will generally be looking for value for money, but the price you can charge will depend on several factors. If customers have a perception that your business is rather special and 'up-market' they are more likely to be prepared to pay a higher price. If you are competing with other similar local businesses, your prices must be in line with your competitors. Changes in income can also have an effect. For example, if taxes or interest rates were to be raised then customers would have less money in their pockets. They would be less inclined to spend money and you might have to lower your prices to encourage them to spend.

Level of quality/service

Your customers might be attracted to your business because it offers a high-quality service with regular and frequent deliveries. Are you going to be able to maintain the service if you are sick and unable to work? If you are offering an after-sales service, what days and times would your customers need the service? Would you have to be prepared to work evenings and weekends in order to visit customers who were at work during the day?

How often are your customers likely to want to buy from you? If you are selling a product that has a long lifespan, your customers will not normally be buying the product regularly. Therefore you will need to attract customers from a wide area. On the other hand, if you are selling fresh produce then your customers are more likely to come back regularly; in this case a business relying on the local market might be profitable.

Figure 4.1 For your business to be successful, you need to get the right balance between quality and price

Competition

You should identify other businesses that sell similar products or services, and compare your offerings with theirs. If they sell similar products to you, but to a different market, they may not be competitors as they will not be trying to attract the same customers.

For example, if you had a sandwich business in the town centre another sandwich business operating from a delivery van selling direct to out of town offices would not be a competitor. However, if they opened a shop in the town centre, selling products that could be substituted for yours, then they would be a competitor. Is there room in the market for the two businesses?

Selling

A business must sell its products or services to make an income. That income must exceed all the costs in order for the business to make a profit. There are several ways that you can consider selling your product:

- *In a shop where customers would come to you.* You and your team of sales assistants would help customers to make their choices. You would have to consider the cost of renting the shop and paying staff.
- *By mail order.* You might consider selling your products solely via the Internet, where customers can shop when it suits them. You might also advertise in a magazine or newspaper, particularly if you are trying to make contact with a specific group of readers. These methods would be more successful if you were selling a product that was easy to pack and post. You may be able to rent storage space more cheaply than you could rent shop space.
- *Hand delivery.* If you deliver your goods to customers' homes and businesses (for example, if you had a sandwich round or were selling goods from a catalogue) you would have to consider the transport costs.
- *Service at clients' homes.* If you were offering a service such as cleaning, decorating or building, you might drop leaflets in an area, leaving a telephone number for potential customers to contact you. You might also consider placing advertisements or posters in places such as supermarkets or libraries.

Changing trends and fashions

If your shop stocks fashion items such as clothes, you know that fashion is constantly changing and you must shift your stock quickly to make room for new lines. If you sell food, drink, sweets, and other foods, you have to deal with the shelf life of products and turn the stock over before products reach their sell-by dates. Is your potential market likely to be influenced by issues such as these?

For example, at the time of writing, the latest fashion shows have featured numerous variations on the theme of the 'puff ball' skirt. It is likely that such a distinctive style will be short-lived, so it would be unwise to buy too much stock.

Figure 4.2 A 'puff ball' skirt – how long will it stay in fashion?

Materials and supplies

If you are **selling** a product, you will have to buy in your stock from another business such as the local cash and carry warehouse. A sales representative may call on you, on behalf of a supplier, to persuade you to order more stock and to try new lines. If you are **making** a product, you will need to obtain raw materials and possibly machinery and equipment. If you are offering a service, you will generally not carry much stock – possibly spare parts, stationery, cleaning materials, office equipment and other items you need for your work.

Successful businesses operate on a 'just in time' policy. This means they purchase just enough stock to meet demand, so that they don't have to pay out large sums of money before the goods are sold.

Technology plays a vital role in the modern world to identify the minimum stock levels to achieve the maximum return, without having to turn away dissatisfied customers.

Carrying out market research

In order to find the answers to these questions, a business will carry out **market research**. Successful market research will draw on primary and secondary sources of information.

Primary research will stem from observations you may have made, and from interviews or questionnaires. You should aim to gather information from a sample of people who represent the groups you are hoping to sell to. The larger the sample you interview, the more accurate your research is likely to be, although you must always remember that no survey is perfect and there will always be a margin of error. It would be helpful to look back at the section entitled 'Using surveys' in Unit 1 before you start to design any questionnaire for market research purposes.

Secondary research material can be sourced from published reports that reveal the results of surveys carried out by the Government and other organisations. This material may be available in the form of Government publications, retail audits or reports by key operators in the market, such as retailers, wholesalers and suppliers. In addition, established businesses will have their own sales and customer records. Published research may not have been carried out for exactly the same purpose as you require and you should bear in mind that it may be less useful and reliable than your own research findings.

You must remember to record and acknowledge all sources of information.

Think it over ...

When Thomas Tripp and Barbie Beach first had the idea of opening Travelbug, it was necessary for them to carry out research as to the viability of their venture.

○ How do you think they went about this?

○ Give examples of the questions they may have included in a questionnaire?

Skills Builder

At this stage you should be able to tackle Task 3 of the Skills Builder mini project on page 53. Don't forget to study the scenario carefully so that you are clear about the project objective.

Financial planning

Spreadsheet models

Financial planning is crucial to business success. A successful enterprise needs to identify the flow of income and expenditure, to ensure that costs can be covered. This analysis can then be used to calculate the break-even point and to predict profits. Spreadsheet software is an invaluable tool for creating a computer model of the financial side of a business. The model may be a simple forecast, such as a budget plan for planning an 18th birthday party, or something extremely complicated, such as a model of a school's income and expenditure.

A spreadsheet model to identify the potential break-even and profit points is based on

- different values of input data
- formulas which define the rules of the model
- output data, which will vary according to the values of the input data.

An effective model will consider alternatives and the effect of various actions, such as

- increasing the price of an item to establish how much more income would be generated and how much profit might be made
- the importance of timing to ensure that costs can be met without encountering cash flow problems, and to identify which points in the year have the most expenditure or the lowest income
- varying the source of supplies or the type or quantity of raw materials used, to establish whether expenditure can be reduced.

Using spreadsheet software to design and build models enables you to make decisions such as

- *how much to charge for a product/service* – the more that is charged, the greater the profit may be, but if the product/service becomes too expensive then sales may drop and profit is reduced.
- *how much stock to purchase* – it is important to have enough stock available so that customers are not turned away, but not to be over-stocked so that business capital (money) is tied up. The capital would be better left earning interest in the bank or used to finance new opportunities that arise.
- *how much you need to sell to break even*
- *whether to expand or reduce existing activities*:
  - If an item is selling really well, do you place another large order from the supplier, or is there a risk that the market is saturated and you will be unable to sell the items?
  - If an item that was popular and profitable is no longer selling well, you have to make a decision to continue or to withdraw the line. For example, cold air fans are popular during a heat wave, but do not sell well in cold weather. You may decide not to re-order in October, but still continue the line. On the

Jargon buster

In stock terms a **line** is one particular product for sale.

Skills check ▷▷

As with all the work you prepare for your projects, you must make effective use of the presentation and formatting facilities offered by the software. Refer to the Spreadsheet Software skills section (page 107) for information about using

- font style and size, colours, borders and shading to enhance the layout
- formulas and formatting techniques – such as conditional formatting, linking worksheets, limit data input to acceptable values only, hiding or protecting cells – to ensure the accuracy of the data and the information obtained from it
- charts and graphs to present the results of the model.

other hand, if a new version of a games console is due to be launched within the next month or two then it is good business sense to discontinue the previous model and to wait until the new model is available before placing your next order.

Before you can develop a useful spreadsheet model, you need to decide what

- information you want from the model
- data should be entered
- calculations must be performed
- output is required.

Let's consider a simple spreadsheet model. Travelbug are thinking of offering day trips to France via Eurotunnel, with a meal included. Thomas Tripp wants to know the costs for

- a coach and driver
- fuel
- crossing to France using Eurotunnel
- a meal in France.

He can use this information to decide how much they should charge their customers.

Barbie Beach has established that the fixed costs are

- 55 seater coach – £300
- driver's wages – £100
- Fuel – £120
- Eurotunnel – £300
- Food/drink – £500 regardless of the number of people. (This is a good price for the meal provided they sell enough tickets.)

Barbie is considering charging £40 per person. She has created a spreadsheet model to establish the costs, the income and how many customers they will need in order to break even. Figure 4.3 shows the spreadsheet model, giving the total of fixed costs and the variable income depending on the number of tickets sold. You can see that if they charge £40 per person then they must sell 33 seats to break even. If they sell all the seats then they will make a profit of £880.

Notice that the use of suitable font style and size, bold and colour makes the spreadsheet much clearer. The 'If' function was used in row 15 so that the words 'Loss', 'Break Even' or 'Profit' would appear automatically, depending on the values in row 14.

Conditional formatting was used in rows 14 and 15 so that the result would be illustrated in red, blue or green, depending on the values of the data.

Having established the layout of the spreadsheet model, it is a simple matter to try out different values. For example, what if they increase the charge for the day trip to £44 each? Figure 4.4 shows the model after the fare has been increased. This time they need to sell only 30 seats to break even, and if they fill the coach then the profit will increase from £880 to £1100.

Barbie Beach has decided that it is worth trying out the new service, and feels that she can make an introductory offer of £40, but will increase it to £44 for future day trips.

	A	B	C	D	E
1					
2		Day Trip To France			
3					
4	Vehicle - 55 seater	£300			
5	Driver	£100			
6	Fuel	£120			
7	Euro Tunnel	£300			
8	Food/drink	£500			
9	Fixed Costs	£1,320			
10					
11	Fare	£40	£40	£40	£40
12	No of Passengers	15	20	33	55
13	Income	£600	£800	£1,320	£2,200
14	Profit/Loss	-£720	-£520	£0	£880
15		Loss	Loss	Break Even	Profit

Figure 4.3 A spreadsheet model of the costs and income to run a day trip to France

	A	B	C	D	E
1					
2		Day Trip To France			
3					
4	Vehicle - 55 seater	£300			
5	Driver	£100			
6	Fuel	£120			
7	Euro Tunnel	£300			
8	Food/drink	£500			
9	Fixed Costs	£1,320			
10					
11	Fare	£44	£44	£44	£44
12	No of Passengers	15	20	30	55
13	Income	£660	£880	£1,320	£2,420
14	Profit/Loss	-£660	-£440	£0	£1,100
15		Loss	Loss	Break Even	Profit

Figure 4.4 A spreadsheet model of the costs and income to run a day trip to France, showing an alternative fare price

The data can also be illustrated as a line graph. This style of graph is most suitable to illustrate a break-even point. This is the point where the fixed costs and the income meet, and is clearly visible in Figure 4.5.

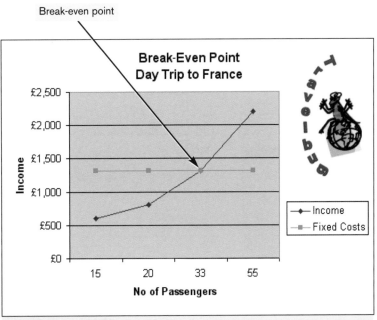

Figure 4.5 Line graph showing the break-even point for a day trip to France

Testing

There is a great danger of assuming that results produced using a computer must be right. It is essential to check that your spreadsheet model is accurate. There may be an error in one of the formulas, or the data type may be unsuitable. For example, should a numerical value be set to *integer* (whole number) or *decimal*? When the model is first designed, enter test data and then check the results using a calculator. For example, in the model shown in Figure 4.3, you could multiply the number of passengers by the cost of the fare, and confirm that the total income is correct.

The use of validation rules helps to ensure the accuracy of a model. There is a range of validation criteria available (Figure 4.6). For example, the cells containing the number of passengers were each set to be a whole number with a maximum of 55, as there are only 55 seats in the coach. If you then enter a number higher than 55, an error message appears warning you that the value you entered is not valid. Obviously it is still possible to make data entry errors, but setting a data validation rule reduces the risk of mistakes.

Figure 4.7 Setting data validation

Figure 4.6 Validation criteria

Figure 4.8 Validation error message

Go out and try!

The day trips to France have proved very successful, so Travelbug have had the idea of running a coach trip to London theatres. The coach seats 60 people and the block booking for the theatre tickets is £1,500. The cost of the coach is £400, and they calculate that the cost of the fuel will be £60 and the coach driver will cost £80 for the evening. They intend to sell the tickets for £60 each.

1 Design a spreadsheet model to find out
   ○ the minimum number of tickets they need to sell to break even
   ○ how much profit they will get if they sell all the seats
   ○ what the effect would be of increasing the ticket cost to £70

2 Think about where you could use validation rules to limit data entry errors.

3 Test the accuracy of the spreadsheet by checking the results.

Start a file called 'ICT and Enterprise'. Create a new bold heading called '**Spreadsheet models**' and describe the skills you have learnt.

Skills Builder

At this stage you should be able to tackle Tasks 4 and 5 of the Skills Builder mini project on page 54. Don't forget to study the scenario carefully so that you are clear about the project objective.

Creating a marketing plan

You should prepare a marketing or business plan to show that you have thought about the way you are going to develop your business. The information you have researched will form the basis of your marketing plan. Marketing plans may vary depending on the type of organisation and the reason they are being prepared. However, all marketing plans will include the '**4Ps**' of marketing:

- Product – a description of the products and/or services
- Place – where they are sold and how they will be distributed
- Price – how much is to be charged
- Promotion – how they will be promoted.

Your marketing plan may follow the structure in the table below:

Enterprise aim	Short-term and long-term aims of the enterprise.
Current position	Analysis of the market and the potential customers: • Identify any competitors • Is there a unique selling point? • Which resources are available and which do you need to obtain?
Marketing targets	For example, how many products do you expect to sell in the first year?
Marketing mix	Give details here of the 4Ps of marketing referred to above.
Marketing strategy	How do you intend to market (inform the public about) your product?
Summary and conclusions	Summarise the main features of the whole marketing plan.

Presenting business proposals

If you are to be successful with a new enterprise, it is imperative that you are able to communicate your ideas effectively. You will need to learn to use presentation software, such as PowerPoint, to convey information in a professional way.

Have you ever attended a presentation where the speaker merely reads his notes or the text on slides word for word? If you have, you will know that this is not an effective way of communicating information, as the presentation will be very dull and boring. You will need, therefore, to think about the best way of presenting information; for example, you might use the text on each slide to jog your memory so that you can elaborate and give further details on each point.

Skills check ▶▶

You will learn how to create presentations using PowerPoint in the skills chapter on page 126.

The presenter of a successful business presentation will have taken the time to design slides that convey the main points clearly.

Content and Structure

In the same way as when you are creating a website or other multimedia product, you will need to plan the content and structure. Creating a storyboard and structure chart is essential before you start building the slides.

You will need to make decisions about the multimedia components you want to include; for example text, graphics, sounds, video, animation, charts or diagrams. Remember that having too many different components can take the focus off the overall aim of a presentation – don't use a component such as animation just to show off your new skills; use it only if it adds to the overall content and message you want to convey. The position on the page of key items is also very important – if you do not give much thought to this, the overall impression can be messy.

Finally, you should pay attention to the proportion of text to any visual or audio information. Often it is easier to convey a message using images rather than blocks of text.

⦿ Think it over ...

Compare the two slides in Figure 4.9. The content is exactly the same, but the positioning of the components is different. Which do you think has the most effective layout and why?

Cruise Club

- Services of our specially trained staff
- 2 for 1 cruise offers
  - Monthly newsletter
- Specially discounted rates
  - Cabin upgrades

Cruise Club

- Services of our specially trained staff
- 2 for 1 cruise offers
  - Monthly newsletter
  - Specially discounted rates
  - Cabin upgrades

Figure 4.9 Position of components on a slide

Presentation techniques

Layout, font type and size

In the presentation skills section you will learn how to lay out each slide either using the PowerPoint design templates or by building a slide from scratch. When choosing the font and size, remember that you will need to ensure that people at the back of the audience can read the slides, so do not use too small a font – 24 point or above is a good size.

You also need to consider the **x-height** of a font: the height of the lower-case x, and of many other lower-case letters such as a, c and e. Two fonts may both be the same point size but have different x-heights.

Look at the following two lines of text, both of which are in 16-point fonts:

This text is in 16-point Arial

This text is in 16-point Verdana

Line spacing and alignment

You can use the same skills that you use in word processing to change the line spacing of text (for example from single to double) and its alignment (centred, justified and so on).

Bullets

You can easily create bulleted lists with PowerPoint. Bullet points are helpful when used as prompts and to summarize points.

Text wrapping

PowerPoint allows you to word wrap text in an AutoShape. To do this you need to ensure that the **Word wrap text in AutoShape** checkbox is selected in the *Format AutoShape* dialogue box, as shown in Figure 4.10.

Thomas Tripp selected this option for the final slide of his PowerPoint presentation (Figure 4.11).

Figure 4.10 Format AutoShape dialogue box

Figure 4.11 Word wrapping text in an AutoShape

Colour and backgrounds

You will need to consider the colour scheme for your presentation. The Presentation Software skills chapter (page 126) covers how to change such things as the colours used for text and lines, shadows, title text, fills, accents, hyperlinks and backgrounds.

TiP

Use colours carefully; remember that if you change the colour scheme from slide to slide, it will take the audience time to adjust. It is acceptable to change the colour on one slide in order to draw special attention to the slide, or to break a long presentation into appropriate chunks with a different colour scheme for each chunk, but never change the colour scheme without a specific purpose.

Take the following design considerations into account when creating a presentation.

- You should choose text and background colour combinations carefully, and go for high contrast. If you choose a subtle difference, the text may be difficult to read. Also, if the data projector cannot handle these slight differences, both the text and background colours may default to the same colour!
- You need to consider the environment where you will be giving the presentation. A dark background with light text is best for dark rooms, whereas a light background with dark text is best for light rooms.
- You will see from Figure 4.12 that you should avoid patterned backgrounds behind text – the text is almost impossible to read!

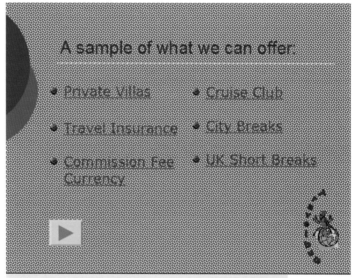

Figure 4.12 Example slide with a patterned background

Transitions

When you show a PowerPoint presentation, you can apply different slide transitions when you move from one slide to the next. When you design a PowerPoint presentation, each slide has a transition associated with it. PowerPoint offers a large number of different transition styles to choose from – for example *box in*, *box out*, *blinds horizontal* and *blinds vertical*. If you prefer, you can set the slide transition to *no transition*. Any special effects should be used with care – they should be used to enhance your presentation, so take care that they do not distract or irritate.

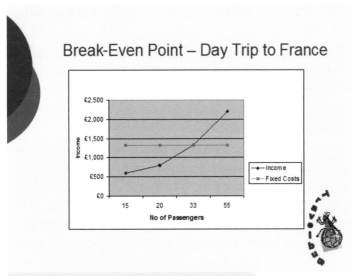

Figure 4.13 Inserting a graph into a presentation

Transferring information

One useful feature of PowerPoint is that you can include information in a slide from another software application. For example, you can insert a table produced in a word processor into a slide. When Thomas Tripp and Barbie Beach were forming Travelbug, they created a presentation to show their bank manager. As you can see in Figure 4.13, they were able to copy a graph produced in Excel and paste it into a slide.

Delivering the presentation

You should prepare for a presentation by doing the following things.

- *Rehearsing what you are going to say.* PowerPoint allows you to record the narration so that you can check what the presentation will sound like to an audience. You can do this by choosing the **Record Narration** option from the **Slide Show** menu (Figure 4.14). Having recorded what you want to say, you can run the presentation and sit back and listen. You will find that you get an entirely different point of view when you pretend to be the audience. You will find it easier to pick up any unclear passages, boring aspects or any awkward moments.

Figure 4.14 Record Narration dialogue box

Having made any changes, you can simply turn off the narration by choosing **Set Up Show** from the **Slide Show** menu and selecting the **Show without narration** option.

- *Checking timings, transitions and content.* As well as rehearsing what you are going to say, you should check any timings carefully. You need to estimate how long it will take you to present a slide, or how long you need between animations on a slide. By choosing **Rehearse Timings** from the **Slide Show** menu you can ensure that you do not have to speak too rapidly or too slowly when doing your final presentation.

○ *Checking your content carefully.* There is nothing worse than realising halfway through a presentation that you have spelt a word incorrectly, and it will not create a very good impression!

Producing speaker notes and handouts

You will learn in the Presentation skills section on page 139 how to create speaker notes; this feature allows you to include notes with a slide. You can add anything you want in these notes, and the slides can be printed out with the notes. Thomas Tripp can use this facility to give extra details on the different cities shown on the City Break slide of his presentation. He can print out the slide, together with the notes, to give to prospective customers.

No one in the audience will realise that you have included speaker notes, unless you print them out as handouts, so you can use them for reminders about what you want to say. When you are running the presentation, if you right-click on the slide with speaker notes and select **Speaker Notes** from the menu, the *Speaker Notes* dialogue box will appear, but will not be seen by the audience (Figure 4.15). You can even edit the notes during a show!

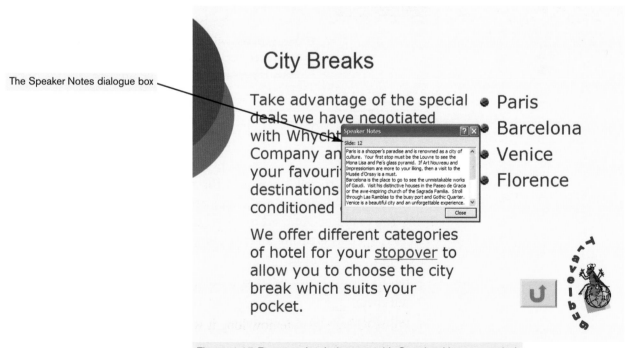

Figure 4.15 Presentation being run with Speaker Notes revealed

Finally, it is useful to be able to give your audience handouts either at the beginning or the end of the presentation. You can choose to print three slides on each page, with a space on the right-hand side for notes (Figure 4.16); it is useful for an audience to receive these handouts at the outset so that they can write their own notes whilst you are presenting.

Figure 4.16 Printing handouts

If you are trying to sell a new idea for an enterprise, you need to ensure that you hold your audience's attention rather than distract them. You could be tempted to spend time using all the features available, such as creating a fancy animation, whilst forgetting the basic rules of presenting:

- tell to the audience what you are going to tell them
- tell them
- tell what you have told them.

A first-class presentation will be of little use if, when you come to deliver it, you are ill-prepared or a poor presenter.

Skills Builder

At this stage you should be able to tackle Tasks 6 and 7 of the Skills Builder mini project on page 53. Don't forget to study the scenario carefully so that you are clear about the project objective.

Creating a corporate identity

The first thing most people conjure up in their mind when talking about well-known companies or products is a vision of the brand image. For this reason, it is of the utmost importance that a business establishes a recognisable corporate image or identity. The corporate identity encompasses all aspects of the business: packaging, stationery, websites, fleets of delivery vehicles, publications and even the uniform worn by employees. Millions of pounds are spent every year by businesses promoting their brand image or corporate identity.

A brand image may be based on a name, a logo or a particular colour. Football clubs are big business and they are instantly recognised from their name, logo and team colours. For example the colour we associate with Chelsea is blue, whereas with Manchester United it is red. If you think of easyJet, the budget airline, the colour orange will spring to mind; Virgin products and services are associated with red.

You will develop a corporate identity or brand image for your business enterprise. You must decide on the type of image you want your business to have, such as trendy, efficient, high-tech, stylish, environmentally friendly or customer focussed. When designing your brand image you will need to think about a logo and strap-line, a colour scheme, and the format and style you want to use.

Logo

Your logo should make your business easily recognisable. It may be formed from the initials of the business name, or you may choose a simple image to represent the business. The logo should be clear and uncomplicated. If you have already studied Unit 3, you will be familiar with the website LogoLounge (available via http://www.heinemann.co.uk/hotlinks (express code 9850P)) which showcases the work of many top graphic designers. If not, it would be a good idea to browse the website for ideas before you embark on your logo design.

Strap-line

A *strap-line* is a snappy little phrase that businesses use to let people know what their business is about. For example, Travelbug use the strap-line 'Your holiday is in safe hands'. You will need to think of a suitable strap-line to represent your business enterprise, and you might use a strap-line to emphasise an aspect of your business that you are trying to promote, such as the environment, value for money or personal service.

Figure 4.17 The Royal Institute of Chartered Surveyors incorporate a strapline that describes the principles they represent

Colour scheme

Assessment Hint

You will probably experiment with a variety of colour combinations as you develop your ideas; you must remember to keep your early design work as evidence for your e-portfolio.

The colours in your logo will usually be reused throughout the business. When considering colour, you should bear in mind that whatever you choose will probably be used for both printed and on-screen publications. For example, the logo will be used on letterheads, business cards, brochures and web pages. You may decide to select one colour from the logo to be used for text and another colour for the background. You must make sure there is sufficient contrast between the background and foreground colours so that any text can be read easily either on a screen or in print.

Black and white can be very effective, a combination of grey and white can look stylish and modern, and green is associated with the environment.

Format and style

Your choice of font style and size is also an important consideration. A consistent approach gives the impression of a well-organised business. You may decide to adopt a particular font style and colour for the business name and a different style for other details. You

Think it over ...

Look at a range of company websites and consider the following:

- Does the overall image reflect the nature of the business?
- Is the logo easily identifiable?
- Is a strap-line used to communicate what the company does?
- Does the house style reflect the colours used in the logo?

should make sure that the font style you choose is suitable for both print and screen, and that it is accepted by different browsers. Don't choose something too flamboyant unless you are promoting a showy, colourful business image. A more modest approach will generally be taken more seriously.

Business Communication

Templates

An initial impression of any business is usually formed from the way that it communicates. For example, an unhelpful employee at the end of a telephone does little to promote the image of the business.

Figure 4.18 What sort of impression does this give to customers?

In the same way, poorly presented documentation does nothing to enhance the image of the business. To ensure that all correspondence sent from any department in the organisation looks the same, businesses use templates that reflect their house style. Templates are frequently used for letters, faxes, invoices, receipts, business cards, and other customer documents.

One advantage of using a template is that every time you open it, the layout and style of the document is ready for you to use straight away. You do not have to spend time changing font styles, margins, text alignment, and so on.

For your project, you will create a series of templates for standard business documents. You will need to consider the purpose of each template when creating its content and structure. Your templates should all reflect your chosen corporate identity. For example, each template should include the logo and use the same font style and colour, although the size of font will probably vary between templates. Wherever possible, common components, such as the business address, should be displayed in a similar position to give an overall impression of consistency in layout.

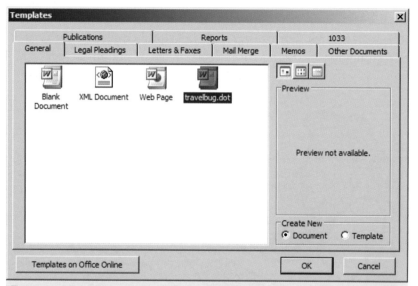

Figure 4.19 Templates are stored under the General tab in the Templates window

When you are satisfied with the design of each template, you should test it in two ways. First, use it to prepare a document for which it was designed. Make sure you are able to complete it in the way you intended – that all the information fits in the right place. Second, show your design to other people for their comments and, if necessary, modify your design to take account of their feedback. When you are sure your design is complete, you must save it as a template file. Templates created in Word take the file extension **.dot** and templates created in Excel become **.xlt**. They will automatically be saved in the *General* template folder and can be identified as templates by the yellow band on the icon.

A document created from a template will be saved with a normal extension (**.doc** or **.xls**). Adding content to the new document will not change the template, which will be ready next time you need it.

Business letterhead

A business letterhead is used for written communications that are sent outside the business. Because the letterhead will be sent to customers and suppliers, and may even be their first form of contact with the business, it must be designed to reflect the business's corporate identity.

✓ TiP

To ensure that the positions of text and images on your letterhead are not affected when you use the template to prepare letters, it is a good idea to create the letterhead in **Header and Footer** view. On screen the colours will appear to be dull when you write a letter based on the template, but when you print it the colours will be as you created them.

A letterhead will usually include

- a logo
- the name of the business
- the full address, including the post code
- the telephone number
- a fax number, where applicable
- an email address
- the website URL.

When you design the letterhead for your business enterprise, you must think about where you will place the logo, company name and address, and other components on the page. Since the purpose of a letterhead is to provide space for a letter to be written, you should aim to make as much white space available as possible. Therefore, to maximise usable space, make full use of the top and bottom margin areas for the business information. In addition, think about margin size, your corporate colours and the font style and size you will use to make your letterhead effective.

17 London Road   Whychton   **TO9 3WN**
Tel: 543 2134 5678   www.travelbug.co.uk
Fax: 543 2134 5679   Email: info@travelbug.co.uk

Figure 4.20 The Travelbug letterhead maximises the use of white space

17 London Road   **Whychton**   **TO9 3WN**
Tel: 543 2134 5678   www.travelbug.co.uk
Fax: 543 2134 5679   Email: info@travelbug.co.uk

Our Ref TT/BB

18 October 2005

The Manager
Nationwide Hotel Group
123 London Road
HEATHWOOD
LL5 BB3

Dear Sir

NEW BUSINESS VENTURE

Travelbug is an independent holiday company and we are planning to diversify into the area of coach touring holidays. We would like to establish a network of hotels to link into our itineraries.

Your group has hotels close to many of the attractions we will be including in our tours and we would like to discuss the possibility of arranging block bookings with you.

In order to explore this possibility in detail I would like to propose a meeting with you in the course of the next few weeks. I enclose a copy of our company brochure for your information

I will telephone you early next week to arrange a mutually convenient date.

Yours faithfully

Thomas Tripp
Director

Enc

Figure 4.21 A letter presented on Travelbug's letterhead

In Unit 1 we looked at the style of presentation used for business letters. We found that most businesses adopt a fully blocked style of presentation, where all text starts at the left-hand margin and the only punctuation used is included for grammatical purposes. When you prepare business letters on your new letterhead, make sure you refer back to Unit 1 to remind yourself of the information that you should include in your letter. You must also make sure that the writing style and tone are suitable for the purpose of the letter.

Fax cover sheet

A *facsimile message* – or *fax* – is used to send a copy of a document over a telephone line. The document is converted into electronic signals, which are transmitted through the telephone system. The signals are converted back into a copy of the original document and printed on the receiving fax machine.

?

Think it over ...

Look at the various fax template styles that are available in your word processing software. Which do you prefer? What changes would you need to make to a standard template if you wanted to use it for your business?

Some computer systems have fax software, which overrides the need for a fax machine. The fax is sent from the computer to a fax machine or computer at the other end. Faxes received are displayed on the computer screen.

A document sent by fax may have any number of pages, and can contain text and images. However, so that the person receiving the fax knows what is being sent, from whom and how many pages have been sent, a fax cover sheet is usually sent first.

A fax cover sheet will include

- a logo and strap-line
- the name and full details of the company sending the fax
- the name, fax and telephone numbers of the person to receive the fax
- the name, fax and telephone numbers of the person sending the fax
- today's date
- the number of pages being sent (including the cover sheet)
- the subject heading
- space for a short message.

The telephone numbers are included so that the person receiving the fax can be contacted to say the message has been sent. If there is a problem and only part of the message is received, the person sending the fax can also be contacted and asked to resend it. Any message included on the fax cover sheet is usually quite brief and informal, whereas the document that is being attached may be written in a more formal style and tone.

The fax cover sheet that you design for your business should reflect the corporate identity in the same way as your letterhead. It can be helpful to use a table to display the information that you wish to include. Borders and shading can be used effectively to improve the appearance of the table.

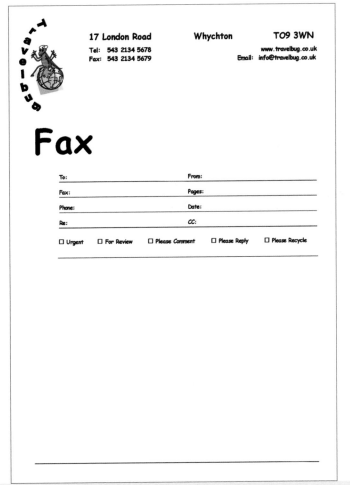

Figure 4.22 Travelbug's Fax Cover Sheet clearly reflects the corporate identity

Invoice

An invoice is sent to a customer requesting payment for goods or services supplied. It will list the individual items that have been sent to the customer and will show the cost of each item and the overall value of the invoice. Each invoice is given a unique reference number.

The appearance of the invoice will reflect the corporate identity in the same way as a letterhead or fax. It will include the following details:

- the logo and strap-line
- full details of the company, including name, address and telephone number
- space for customer's name, address and account number
- the invoice number
- the date
- the supplier's VAT number, if they have one
- details of goods supplied – typically *quantity*, *reference*, *description* and *unit price*
- the total cost of the invoice, including goods and services, VAT, postage and packing charges, and anything else the customer is being charged for
- terms and conditions for settling the invoice.

Skills check ▷▷

Refer to the skills section on Spreadsheet software (page 107) for information about using the formatting tools.

You will prepare your invoice in spreadsheet software so that you can build in formulas to calculate the cost of each item and the total cost of the invoice. You can remove the gridlines from the spreadsheet and include borders and shading where you think they are necessary. In this way your invoice will be clear to read and the totals will stand out.

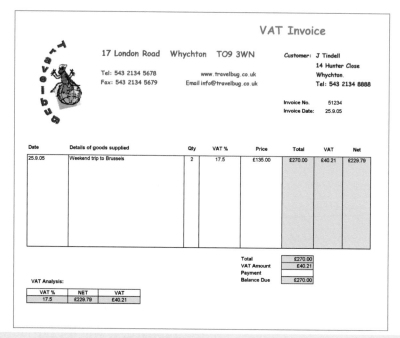

Figure 4.23 This is the invoice Travelbug use to confirm holiday bookings. It has been designed to suit the purpose of the business. In this case the details of goods supplied refers to holiday bookings and the quantity indicates the number of people

Receipt

If you were running a business that took in customers' personal belongings to repair them, you may give the customer a receipt to confirm that the goods are in your possession.

For example, a jeweller repairing some earrings will give the customer a receipt with a receipt number. The item of jewellery will also be allocated the same number, so the jeweller can match the item with the receipt when the customer calls to collect it. The customer must produce the receipt in order to collect the goods. Without the receipt, the jeweller has no way of knowing for certain that the item actually belongs to the person claiming it.

The receipt is usually in two sections – one for the business and one for the customer. It may be perforated to allow the two sections to be separated easily.

Another use for a receipt is to confirm that a payment has been received. If you buy something in a supermarket, you are given a receipt printed from the till. This lists the items you have bought and how much you paid for them. If you buy expensive products from other types of shops, you will also be given a receipt to confirm that you have paid for the goods; this receipt may be handwritten or printed from a computer document. Sometimes the receipt confirms that you have paid a deposit at the time of ordering goods, and that there is still an outstanding balance to be paid before the goods are delivered. The exact details on a receipt will vary depending on the purpose of the receipt, but typically will include

- the logo and strap-line
- a receipt number
- the date
- the name and full details of the business
- the name and full details of the customer, including telephone number
- a brief description of the goods for repair and an indication of the problem, or a description of the product or service paid for
- an indication of the cost of repair or the amount of money paid
- the name or initials of the person accepting the repair.

Go out and try!

Design two receipts:
○ one that can be given to customers when they take electrical goods in for repair
○ one that can be given to customers when they pay for the repair.

Open your file called 'ICT and Enterprise'. Create a new bold heading called '**Designing receipts**' and describe the skills you have learnt.

Business cards

If you are browsing round a retail store and you stop to ask a sales assistant for some advice, it is likely that the sales assistant will offer you his or her business card before you leave the store. When people look at new cars in a showroom, or arrange for a salesperson to call at home to discuss a new kitchen or replacement windows, they will also be offered a business card by the salesperson.

The sales staff have realised that there is a potential sale, and they are anxious to ensure that the customer doesn't forget which salesperson was helping them. Many sales staff rely on commission from the goods they sell to boost their salaries, so it is important to them that customers feel they have received a personal service and want to come back to the same assistant.

Most businesses ensure that all staff who come into contact with the public have a supply of business cards to give away. The purpose of a business card is therefore to make sure a business or salesperson is not forgotten and to make it easy for potential customers to get in touch again.

Figure 4.24 A business card should be memorable

A business card measures approximately 8.5 cm × 5.5 cm – just large enough to contain essential information but small enough to fit into a customer's wallet. The details on a business card will usually include

- the logo and strap-line
- the name and address of the business
- the name and job title of the person giving the card together with his/her office and mobile telephone numbers and e-mail address.

The business card will reflect the corporate identity of the business and will usually make use of white space to make it easy for the customer or client to find specific information.

Using your templates

Once your templates are saved in their final versions, you will be able to use them to prepare a variety of letters, invoices, faxes and other business documents. The overall appearance of the documents you produce is very important in order to create a good impression of the business. You should remember to use the various presentation techniques you learnt about in Unit 1 to make your documents readable and professional.

- Use headings and sub-headings to highlight different sections within the document.
- Lay your documents out so that they are clear to read, use paragraphs to break the text up into readable chunks and use white space to help your presentation. You do not have to use every single line that is available on a page.
- Ensure that the font style and size remain the same throughout the document.
- Vary the line spacing to make sections of text stand out, for example in long lists of descriptions and prices. It can be easy to read the wrong price alongside an item if the text is spaced too closely together.
- Use bullet points to identify items in a list.
- Use tables, borders and shading to present information more clearly.
- Choose an appropriate writing style and tone to suit the purpose of the document.
- Proofread every document and don't forget to use the spellchecker too!

Skills Builder

At this stage you should be able to tackle Task 8 of the Skills Builder mini project on page 53. Don't forget to study the scenario carefully so that you are clear about the project objective.

Using email effectively

You will learn in the advertising and promotion section of this chapter (page 44) that modern businesses are making extensive use of email to market their goods and services. Furthermore, email has replaced the internal memo and is now the principal method of communication within organisations.

Anyone that uses email (and fax, telephone, text and picture messaging) to send direct marketing messages must comply with the Privacy and Electronic Communications (EC Directive) regulations 2003. This law was introduced in order to reduce the problem of spam (unsolicited commercial email). Recommended best practice when using email for marketing includes the following:

- Ensure at the point of collection (often on an order form) that it is clearly stated that the email address will be used for marketing.
- Give the person the opportunity to refuse permission for this to be done.
- If the email is to be sent to existing customers, the content of the email should be in respect of similar products and services.
- If the email address is to be shared with a third party, this should be clearly stated.
- Email addresses should not be 'harvested', for example copied from lots of websites.
- If you have received a marketing email, you should be able to refuse permission for further emails to be sent to you. Therefore there should be a clear and simple way of opting out from receiving future emails (see Figure 4.26).

TiP

Think carefully before clicking any links, even 'unsubscribe' ones, sent by businesses you have not had any dealings with. These links might not be legitimate – you might start to get more, not less, spam if you click them!

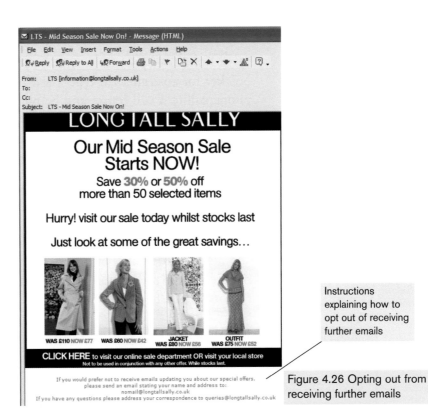

Instructions explaining how to opt out of receiving further emails

Figure 4.26 Opting out from receiving further emails

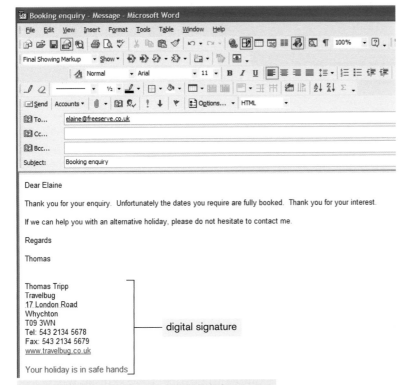

digital signature

Figure 4.27 Example of a formal digital signature

Digital Signatures

When using an email for communication, whether internally or externally, it is good practice to add a digital signature to your message. Most email software will allow you to set up more than one, which has the advantage that you can use a more formal digital signature for external emails, a less formal signature for internal emails and an informal signature for emails to friends and family. Thomas Tripp has used the full contact details, including the Travelbug strap-line 'your holiday is in safe hands', as his external contact digital signature (Figure 4.27).

Automated responses

Most businesses provide an email option for contact because it is quicker for customers to type a few lines via email than to make a phone call to a call centre and be put in a queue. One negative aspect of this is that a business may be swamped with large numbers of emails and, as a result, it may take several days for them to respond to a request, which can lead to customer dissatisfaction.

To respond more quickly, many companies are using the features of email software to set up automated responses to email enquiries. Automatic responses can be used for such things as requests for additional information, requests to have a forgotten password sent and acknowledgement of orders. Companies find that they can handle a large proportion of their emails using automated email responses (see Figure 4.28).

> ✓ **TiP**
>
> *It is not advisable to set up an automatic response saying that you are going to be away on holiday for your personal email account. This is because it can advertise the fact that your home may be empty and therefore open to burglars.*

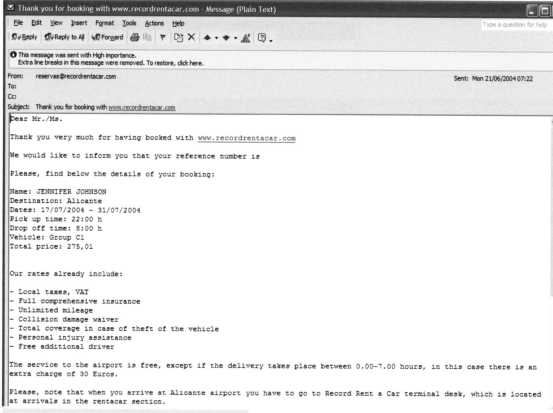

Figure 4.28 Example automated response email

Automatic responses are also useful for individual employees to set up when they are going to be out of the office, for example when they are going on holiday.

Distribution lists

A *distribution list* (sometimes referred to as a *group*) allows you to send an email to a number of email contacts simultaneously, without having to type all the email addresses in the To: box. Businesses find this a useful tool, as they can set up distribution lists for specific purposes; this can save a considerable amount of staff time. For example, as you can see in Figure 4.29, Travelbug use a distribution list to send electronic newsletters to all customers on a monthly basis.

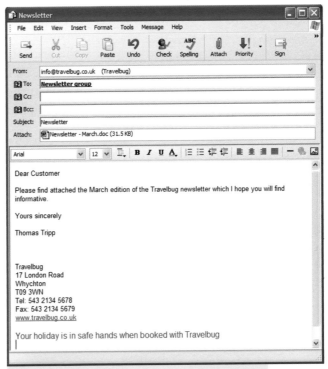

Figure 4.29 Sending an email to a distribution list

Attachments

Skills check ▶▶

Refer to page 163 for detailed information about sending emails with attachments.

You can easily attach one or more files to an email. The email can be sent to one email contact or to a large number of people. You can attach any file, although you need to be aware that emails with large attachments may be blocked by the receiving mail server. It may be necessary to use compression techniques, such as creating a zip file, to send large files. Organisations find emails with attachments to be a quick and economic way to send such things as newsletters, leaflets and brochures. Not only do businesses save time, but they do not have to pay for the printing or postage costs. In Figure 4.29 above, you will see that Thomas Tripp attached the March newsletter to the email sent to the Newsletter distribution group.

Figure 4.30 An example of a poster displayed outside a shop in order to entice customers into the shop!

Advertising and promotion

Businesses must promote the goods or services they supply, both to inform existing customers and to persuade potential customers that this is a product or service they need. Sometimes, special offers are used to entice new customers. For example, you will often see supermarkets with posters saying 'buy one get one free' or 'three for the price of two'. These offers are often heavily advertised in order to get customers in the shop. Once in the shop, customers are likely to buy more than they originally came in for.

Advertisements in magazines, newspapers and on hoardings are a favourite way of catching the attention of customers. Passers-by can also easily see posters in shop windows. Some large companies use sponsorship as a means of advertising, and many sporting teams, both amateur and professional, are willing to display a company logo on their kit in return for sponsorship money.

You will produce a variety of promotional material for your business, including

- advertisements
- leaflets
- posters/flyers
- mail shots
- websites.

When designing these items, you must also consider

- *Structure* – for example, if you are producing a leaflet, will you have one or two folds? What size will you choose for a poster compared to a flyer? Will you opt for portrait or landscape page orientation?
- *Composition* – what components will you include: photographs, images, text?
- *Balance* – how much of the available space will be taken up with text, images or white space? Will the size of one overpower the others?

? Think it over ...

Think about what makes you look twice at an advertisement or poster. What is the first thing to grab your attention? Is it the colours, the words or a particular image? Promotional material must make an impact otherwise nobody will stop to look at it or read it.

○ *Colour* – this will depend very much on where you will be publishing the material. Posters are generally more eye-catching in colour, but advertisements in newspapers can be very effective in black and white. Flyers might be more economical to produce in just two or three different colours. Will the use of colour enhance the product or service you are promoting?

○ *Message* – what is the message you are trying to get across? Make sure you choose an appropriate style and tone. Keep your words to a minimum so they grab the attention of passers-by. Think of promotional words and phrases that catch your attention, such as 'Free', 'Special Offer' and '3 for the price of 2'.

○ *Corporate image* – follow the design principles you applied to the templates you produced for business communications. Be proud of your company name and logo. The more often people see them, the more familiar they will become. Finally, remember to include details of how and where customers can contact you?

SPECIAL OFFER

£75 per person

Valentine's Day in Paris

Romantic dinner for two
Guided tour of the city
including
Cruise on the River Seine

Luxury coach leaves Whychton on 14 February
at 0715, returning 0145.

Please contact us using the details below or return the form.

17 London Road   **Whychton**   **TO9 3WN**

Tel: 543 2134 5678   www.travelbug.co.uk
Fax: 543 2134 5679   Email: info@travelbug.co.uk

Your holiday is in safe hands

Please return to Travelbug, 17 London Road, Whychton, TO9 3N

Name ....

Address ....

....

Telephone ....   Email ....

Please send me full details of the Valentine's Day coach trip to France.

Travelbug would like to contact you again in the future regarding special offers and travel deals. If you are happy for us to do so please tick the box.   ☐

Figure 4.31 This is a flyer Travelbug delivered to homes in the local area. They used an image of a red rose as a watermark because red roses are associated with Valentine's Day

At this stage you should be able to tackle Task 9 of the Skills Builder mini project on page 53. Don't forget to study the scenario carefully so that you are clear about the project objective.

Mail shots

Skills check ▷▷

Remember that such marketing information must only be used in accordance with the Data Protection Act (see the Standard Ways of Working section, page 79).

Nowadays, personal details are often obtained when someone has to complete a form, whether on paper or online, which says something like 'if you do not wish to receive further information about products or services please tick here'. Quite often, this box goes unnoticed and your details are added to a database, which can then be used or sold on to other businesses to use for marketing.

> Travelbug would like to contact you again in the future regarding special offers and travel deals. If you are happy for us to do so, please tick the box. ☐

Figure 4.32 These are the words Travelbug used at the foot of the flyer in Figure 4.31

These details are used for mail shots to inform the public about a product or special offer. This is where mail merge is so useful, because a company can easily reach a huge number of potential customers. Many organisations purchase mailing lists in order to reach their potential market.

Skills check ▷▷

See page 105 for more information about using mail merge. This is also covered in detail on pages 132–136 of the DiDA D201 book.

You will use mail merge to produce a sales letter to customers whose personal details are stored in a database. Think carefully about the most appropriate writing style for your letter and ask someone to look at it and give you their comments. Be prepared to modify your letter as a result of their comments.

Technology is increasingly used to market new products and services. Many companies will ask you for an email address as well as a home address. They are then able to use the email address to email promotional material to you automatically. Web technology is also used as a means of advertising and no doubt you have come across 'pop-ups' advertising goods or services, often totally unconnected to the website you are viewing.

? Think it over ...

Working in small groups, gather together a range of promotional material, such as advertisements from newspapers or magazines, leaflets, posters/flyers and screen prints from websites. Consider the following:
- Does the advertisement grab your attention?
- Is it well structured?
- Is the balance of the components effective?
- Is there a clear message?
- Does it include promotional words such as 'special offer'?
- Does it convey the corporate image, including colour schemes?

Skills Builder

At this stage you should be able to tackle Task 10 of the Skills Builder mini project on page 53. Don't forget to study the scenario carefully so that you are clear about the project objective

Promotional website

Since 1998 the number of households in the UK who could access the Internet from home has risen from 9 per cent (2.3 million) in 1998 to 52 per cent (12.9 million) by the end of 2004 (see Figure 4.33).

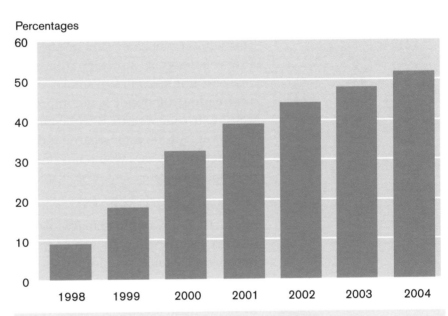

Percentages

Figure 4.33 UK Households with home access to the Internet

Of these people, 61 per cent had used the Internet in the previous three months, and over half of these had bought or ordered goods, tickets or services. (Source: National Statistics website Crown copyright material is reproduced with the permission of the Controller of HMSO.) It is hardly surprising therefore that it is increasingly important for businesses to have a website to promote their products and services. The unique advantages of a website over other forms of marketing include the following:

- Websites are almost always available (except, of course, when the web server on which the website is hosted is unavailable for possible maintenance or there are problems on the Internet itself).

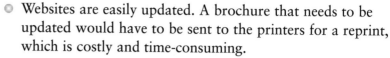

Skills check ▷▷

Refer to the Web Authoring Software chapter (page 170) for information about how to design and build a website.

- Websites are easily updated. A brochure that needs to be updated would have to be sent to the printers for a reprint, which is costly and time-consuming.
- There are low distribution costs. For example, the cost of distributing a brochure includes not only the postage and stationery, but also the staff costs involved in these activities. On the other hand, the cost of ensuring that a website is found easily through Internet searches, and the cost of hosting a website, are far less.

When building and designing a website to promote goods and services, you will need to make decisions on the following aspects.

Number of pages

This will very much depend on the overall content of the website and how you design its structure. You will need to gather the data and then sort it into groups of similar information, discarding any information you decide is not appropriate to the purpose of your website. If your website is for a company promoting travel, such as Travelbug, information regarding the history of travel agencies, although interesting, would not meet the requirements of the overall purpose of the site.

Once you have grouped all the subject matter together, break the information down into manageable chunks. Unlike readers of books, website visitors will scan web pages for the information they require. Keeping the chunks of information relatively small will allow visitors to scan the page easily.

By doing these preliminary tasks you are working towards the organisation and structure of the website.

Content of each page

You will probably decide to structure your website so that each page has a different subject, remembering at all times to keep the data in manageable chunks of bite-sized information. You will also need to consider what graphics, videos or animations will enhance the information.

Also bear in mind download times. If a visitor has to wait a minute for a page to load, they will probably give up. You will therefore need to ensure that any images or videos are compressed in order to enhance download times.

✔ **TiP**

Always ask yourself whether the multimedia elements you are going to use actually add value to the website. If they do not contribute to the website content, leave them out.

The visual design

As well as the content of the website, you need to consider the corporate image and to ensure that there is uniformity between pages. You can use templates and styles to help you achieve this. You will also need to consider colour schemes, fonts styles and sizes, and accessibility issues.

Navigation around the site

A good navigation scheme is extremely important if you want visitors to find the information that they want easily. If they can't navigate their way round a website, they will give up and leave.

You should keep your navigation system the same across the whole website. This means keeping colours, styles and the location of links consistent. It is important to make sure that the Home and Contact links are on every page. Thomas Tripp designed the Travelbug website to ensure that visitors can easily navigate to the home and contact pages (Figure 4.34).

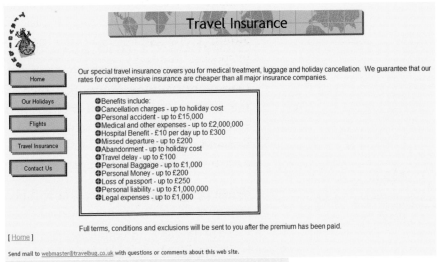

Figure 4.34 Navigation links used by Travelbug website

Contact details

Be aware that some visitors will be very cautious when buying goods or services over the Internet, and will want to check that the company actually exists. There have been many tales of people being taken in by bogus companies advertising on the Internet. Most people will therefore want to know the full telephone number and postal address of the organisation, and could be wary if they can only contact it by email.

For this reason, the Travelbug website includes full contact details (Figure 4.35).

Figure 4.35 Travelbug Contact Us web page

Storyboards and structure charts

Storyboarding is an extremely handy tool for designing the layout and features of multimedia products such as websites. Navigation is one of the most important aspects of website design, for if a visitor cannot find the information they require easily then they may quickly become lost and give up. It is essential to design the navigation of a website and to decide what structure it will take by creating a structure chart.

When designing a website, you will need to produce storyboards and structure charts that show

- the layout and components of each page
- how each page links with the others
- the navigation and structure of the website.

In business, a website developer will always show the initial designs to their client so that they can ensure that the website will be fit for purpose. It is essential that, after you have designed your storyboard and structure chart, you obtain feedback to check that your design meets the requirements of the overall purpose of the website.

Having obtained feedback about the initial designs, and made any necessary adjustments, the website developer will go on to create a working prototype. This will be shown to the customer and once again changes made to ensure that the finished product will meet the customer's needs. Because of the importance of having a suitable website to promote an organisation, any mistakes may be very costly. The testing of the finished website will include ensuring that its functionality is tested in full. This will include testing that

- each page has the correct layout and presentation and the entire site conforms to the corporate style
- all the hyperlinks, both internal and external, work correctly and there are no dead-ends or 'page not founds' (see Figure 4.36)
- all the information is accurate and up to date – for example, it may be a very costly mistake for a company if the website 'contact us' page had an incorrect email address or telephone number
- contact details are available and easy to find
- the site can be viewed in different browsers, and with different types of computer.

ⓘ The page cannot be found

The page you are looking for might have been removed, had its name changed, or is temporarily unavailable.

Please try the following:

- If you typed the page address in the Address bar, make sure that it is spelled correctly.
- Open the www.costablanca-holidays.co.uk home page, and then look for links to the information you want.
- Click the ⇦ Back button to try another link.
- Click Search to look for information on the Internet.

HTTP 404 - File not found
Internet Explorer

Figure 4.36 Example of a 'page not found' page

A web developer will always ask a range of users to test the final prototype to evaluate its usability. The developer will then make any necessary modifications as a result of feedback before the website is finally published on the Internet. A website that is not fully functional and is poorly presented can be very damaging to a business. It is important when you are developing a website that you test it thoroughly.

There are millions of websites on the Internet and every business is keen that their website will be the one that people visit. Publishing a website on the Internet is not sufficient to draw attention to it. Businesses will want to ensure that their websites are listed on search engines; even when a business's website is listed, it will probably be competing against many other websites offering the same goods and services. Often a search will result in thousands of results, and if your site is not listed on the first few pages then it is unlikely that it will be found.

Here are some steps you can take to ensure that a site has a high profile:

- use keywords carefully, so that your pages contain terms that people are likely to search for
- build reciprocal links between external websites – you link to a website and they place a link back to your website
- make sure you have a site map – many search engines like these, as they can visit the whole site from one place
- include 'meta tags' in the html
- ensure that you continuously update your website – some search engines note when a site was last updated.

Meta tags

Meta tags are html code inserted into the beginning (or *head*) of a webpage to describe the website and provide a list of keywords. Some search engines will use meta tags to collect data and list a website. The search engines that do search for meta tags also scan the content of the whole webpage to see if the keywords are repeated.

For example, Thomas Tripp has included the following code in the Travelbug website:

```
<meta name="description" content="Travelbug -
Independent Travel Agency in Whychton">

<meta name="keywords" content="holidays, holiday,
travel agency, independent travel, villas,
cruises, coach trips, holiday insurance">
```

Jargon buster

Keywords refer to the words and phrases most commonly associated with the product or services described in a website. In order to help search engines know what a web page is about, you should use your top keywords six to eight times on a page. If a company sells a number of different services and products, they will need to build individual pages for each set of keywords.

TiP

You can find keyword tools on the Internet which will help you decide the best keywords to use for the product or service you are promoting in your website, for examples, go to www.heinemann.co.uk/hotlinks (express code 9850P)

? Think it over ...

Investigate a number of well known corporate websites to assess their effectiveness as a marketing tool. Consider the following:
- Does the website reflect the corporate style?
- Is the information accurate and up to date?
- Can you navigate easily round it without getting lost?
- Do all the links work?
- Are full contact details provided?

For a website to be successful, it must attract visitors and then entice them to return time and time again.

Skills Builder

At this stage you should be able to tackle Task 11 of the Skills Builder mini project below. Don't forget to study the scenario carefully so that you are clear about the project objective.

Skills Builder mini task

Skills Builder mini task

This activity provides an opportunity to develop the skills you will need in order to complete a summative project for Unit 4. Your teacher may decide to use the tasks in this mini project as further practice as you work through the unit or may set it as a mini project all at once. If it is set as a mini project then, before you begin, you should think about how to plan and manage the project by referring to the Project Planning section (page 199).

Introduction

You have had an idea to organise a leavers' ball. The Principal has suggested that you investigate and make a presentation to her; she will consider agreeing to it if you can show there is enough interest to make your idea viable so that it makes a profit of at least £50, which can be donated to charity. The Principal has indicated that the hall would be made available free of charge.

Your idea was to investigate the possibility of a formal dinner dance with live music or a less formal buffet and disco.

Task 1

Brainstorm ideas with your friends and use mind-mapping software (see page 189) to organise your ideas. Think about the timescales for all the aspects of preparing for the event.

Assessment Hint

Throughout your project, in order to achieve top marks you must
- *create appropriate folder structures*
- *use suitable filenames and file formats*
- *carry out regular back-up procedures.*

Task 2

Prepare a project plan using project planning software (see page 190) and, from this, produce a Gantt chart. You must remember whilst working through this mini-project to modify this plan to take account of any delays that may occur.

Task 3

Design a questionnaire to conduct a survey amongst the top year students to establish
○ how much interest there would be
○ how much they would be prepared to pay
○ what type of music they would like – live band or disco
○ what type of food they would like – sit down dinner or buffet
○ what dress style they would prefer – formal, informal, fancy dress.

Task 4

Analyse the results of your survey using spreadsheet software.

Task 5

Investigate a selection of menus, prices of discos or bands, printing costs for invitations, and other information you might find useful. Prepare a spreadsheet model to illustrate the break-even point.

Task 6

Having considered these various issues, you are now ready to prepare your formal marketing plan. Follow the structure suggested in the text (see page 21).

Task 7

You should now have available all the information you need to prepare your presentation to the Principal. Think about including the following in your presentation:
○ the Gantt chart
○ the financial model

- any charts or graphs produced after analysing your data
- a summary of the marketing plan
- any other relevant information.

Prepare a storyboard and structure chart for your presentation. You should also produce speaker notes and handouts to accompany it.

Task 8

The Principal was very impressed with your presentation and has agreed that the dance can go ahead. You now need to decide on a corporate identity for the event and should design

- a logo
- letterhead and fax templates, including an appropriate strap-line
- the tickets.

Use your fax template to confirm the booking for the band or disco and caterers.

Task 9

Design a poster and flyer to promote the event.

The Principal asked you to make sure that key staff involved in the event are kept informed about it. You have decided that the easiest way to do this is by email. Create a distribution list of five names and send an email to the names on the list, attaching the flyer to check that they are satisfied with the design. You should remember to use a digital signature which includes the strap-line.

Task 10

It has occurred to you that, since the profits are going to charity, you might be able to attract sponsorship from local businesses. Create a database containing the names and addresses of six local businesses who might be willing to sponsor the event. Prepare a mail merge letter on your letterhead to these local businesses describing the event, identifying the charity and asking if they would be willing to sponsor it.

Task 11

Create a website with a minimum of five linked pages to promote the event. You will need to prepare a storyboard and structure chart before implementing your design. Make sure you maintain the corporate design.

Assessment Hint
Tasks 6, 7, 8, 9, 10 and 11

To achieve top marks you must use appropriate structures and styles to ensure that all products are suitable for the target audience, and are the most appropriate way of presenting the information you are trying to get across.

- *Choose an appropriate writing style and tone – formal or informal – and stick to it.*
- *Decide whether to use simple or complex language.*
- *Think about how the information can be most clearly presented – use text, charts and diagrams where appropriate.*
- *Check the products to ensure accuracy – remember to spell check and proofread.*
- *Take account of feedback when modifying the products.*
- *Ensure that evidence of clear planning and appropriate use of components are illustrated in the storyboards and structure charts for the presentation and the website.*
- *Use appropriate speaker notes and handouts to support the presentation.*
- *Make certain that the website's links are effective and the end product is fit for purpose.*

Task 12

When you have finished your project, review your work and produce a short evaluation outlining how well it met the requirements explained in the scenario. Record any aspects you feel could be improved. Justify all of your comments; for example, if you say the corporate design is effective, explain what makes it effective – if something needs changing, explain why and how. You should attach to your evaluation the records of the feedback you received and the actions you took in response.

Task 13

Finally, present your work in an e-portfolio using suitable file formats. Your e-portfolio should be designed to present the following:

- home page
- table of contents
- presentation to be given to the Principal
- poster
- flyer
- mail merge letter produced on the letterhead template
- fax confirming booking
- website.

You should also include some supporting evidence:

- mind map
- project plan
- evidence of data collection using a survey
- questionnaire used for the survey
- spreadsheet showing the survey results including formulas
- references to secondary sources, such as menu prices
- spreadsheet model including formulas
- full marketing plan
- storyboard and structure chart for presentation
- example email and screen print of distribution list
- storyboard and structure chart for the website
- review and evaluation of the project, including feedback from others.

Assessment Hint

You will find that the requirements for the e-portfolio, project planning and review and evaluation are almost identical for each of the units. If you follow the guidelines given in the relevant chapters in the book it will help you achieve top marks.

PART 2

Section 1 | Standard ways of working

While working on your projects you will be expected to use information communication technology (ICT) efficiently, legally and safely. So it is important to understand the need for good practice both in your studies and your future work. The guidelines in this section will ensure that you work with ICT in the correct manner and avoid problems that may cause you to lose your coursework at a crucial stage.

LEARNING OUTCOMES

You need to learn about

✓ file management

✓ personal effectiveness

✓ quality assurance

✓ legislation and codes of practice

✓ working safely.

File management

You may be absolutely brilliant at creating artwork and producing imaginative websites, but is your file management system just as brilliant? If it becomes so disorganised that you cannot remember what a file was called, waste time trying to find the right file, or have no backups, you may not achieve your qualification simply because you were unable to hand in the assignment!

In a work environment, your employer would become frustrated with you if, despite being very capable, you never met your deadlines because of poor file management skills.

So what do you need to do?

- Save work regularly and make backups.
- Use sensible filenames that indicate their contents.
- Use appropriate file formats.
- Set up folder structures.
- Limit access to confidential and sensitive files.
- Use effective protection against viruses.
- Use 'Readme' files where appropriate.

Saving work regularly and making backups

Probably the most obvious and simplest rule to remember is to *save* your work regularly. It is so easy to do, but just as easy to ignore!

You might be so busy designing a superb poster or flyer, thoroughly enjoying working with the graphics and using your imagination, that you forget to save the document. Then, when it is almost finished, you lose *all* the work because there is a power failure or you accidentally delete everything. If you are lucky, when you reopen the application software the file will be 'recovered' by the computer, but you can't guarantee this.

As well as saving your work regularly, it is important to keep backups. Information stored on a computer can be corrupted or lost through a power surge or failure, or by damage to or failure of the hardware. If 'disaster' strikes then you can use the backup copy. It might be slightly out of date, but at least it can be updated.

In business, backups are usually made at the end of every day. At the end of the week another backup is made, and stored separately from the daily backups. To avoid the damage done by viruses or other system-wide disasters, it is not enough to back up files into a different folder on the same computer – files should be regularly backed up onto external storage media. Here are some examples.

- *Floppy disks* are used for fairly small amounts of data – up to 1.4 megabytes (MB). However, files containing graphics quickly become too large to save on a floppy disk.
- *Pen drives*, *flash drives*, *keychain drives* and *memory sticks* (Figure 1) are portable devices that connect to a USB (*universal*

TiP

As soon as you start a new file, save it with a sensible name. After that you can just keep clicking the **Save** icon to update the saved version.

TiP

It is a good idea to keep separate copies of your files each time you make major changes. This way you can record your progress in your e-portfolio. Also, sometimes you decide that an earlier version was better after all, so you can easily go back to it.

Figure 1 Memory stick

serial bus) port of a computer. They can store between 32 MB and 2 GB (gigabytes) of data. These removable drives are the latest method of data storage and are automatically detected by the computer. You can use them to store or move files that won't fit on a floppy disk. These drives are extremely small so they are ideal for transferring files between work or college and home.

- A second hard drive can be installed, either within the same computer or externally. The disadvantage of a second internal drive is that it cannot be stored off-site or in a fireproof safe.

- *Zip drives* are another magnetic disk medium, with storage capacities of up to 250 MB. These are also suitable for domestic or small business use.

- *CD–R* (recordable) and *CD–RW* (re-writable) compact discs can store up to 700 MB. Most modern home PCs are now fitted with built-in CD–RW drives, making this a convenient and inexpensive method of backing up large amounts of data (such as the text and illustrations for this book).

- *DVDs* look the same as CDs, but can store up to 9 GB of data. Several different types of recordable DVD are available.

- A *tape streamer* is a magnetic tape generally used by large businesses. Cartridges that can store up to 300 GB of data are currently available. This method is the most affordable method of backing up the extremely large amounts of data required by large businesses. It also has the benefit that the tapes are small and, as they are removable, they can be stored off-site or in a fireproof safe. The disadvantage of making backup copies on magnetic tapes is that to recover a particular file you must search through the tape starting from the beginning until you reach the file you want – just like with a tape for music.

Jargon buster

One gigabyte (1 GB) equals **approximately** 1000 megabytes. One terabyte (1 TB) equals **approximately** 1000 gigabytes. Text of 500–600 pages uses about 1 MB of space.

Using sensible filenames

When working on any project, *as soon as you have written just a few words on the page*, save the file – naming it in such a way that it is easy to identify later. By having a sensible system for all your filenames, it is easy to find the right one without having to search through (and possibly open) several files.

Older operating systems limited filenames to eight standard characters, but modern operating systems allow more than enough space to identify each file clearly.

With Microsoft operating systems, files usually have more characters, called *extensions*, added to the filename. Filenames are followed by a stop (.) and then an extension of up to three characters. When you save a file, the file extension is usually added automatically to the name you have given the file.

Why is an extension necessary? The extension tells the computer which program to start so that the file can be opened. For example, a Microsoft Word (word processor) document will be followed by **.doc**, an Excel (spreadsheet) file by **.xls**, and a bitmap graphic by **.bmp**. Another important extension is **.exe**, which means an *executable program* – an application. Figure 2 is a list of the most common file extensions.

Extension	Application or type of file
.bmp	Microsoft Paint bitmap image
.doc	Microsoft Word document
.dot	Microsoft Word template
.exe	Executable program
.gif	Graphics interchange format image
.html	Hypertext markup language (web page)
.jpg	Joint Photographic Experts Group (JPEG) image
.mdb	Microsoft Access database
.pdf	Adobe portable document format
.ppt	Microsoft PowerPoint presentation
.pub	Microsoft Publisher publication
.swf	Macromedia Flash vector graphics
.tiff	Tagged image file format image
.tmp	Temporary file
.xls	Microsoft Excel spreadsheet
.xlt	Microsoft Excel template

Figure 2 The most common file extensions

Choosing appropriate file formats

In most cases the file format is automatically selected by the software application. For example, Excel will always use the extension **.xls** for spreadsheets and **.xlt** for templates.

When saving images you often have a choice about which format to use. The screen shots for this book were saved in Corel PhotoPaint and the *TIFF Bitmap* format was chosen (Figure 3) as it allows 16.7 million colours. TIFF graphics are very flexible: they can be any resolution, and can be black and white, greyscale, or full colour. It is the preferred format for desktop publishing as it produces excellent printing results.

Save as type:	TIFF Bitmap (TIF)
	PaintBrush (PCX)
	Targa Bitmap (TGA)
	CompuServe Bitmap (GIF)
Notes:	JPEG Bitmaps (JPG)
	TIFF Bitmap (TIF)
	Adobe Photoshop (PSD)
	Encapsulated PostScript (EPS)
	Portable Network Graphics (PNG)
	Wavelet Compressed Bitmap (WI)
	Kodak FlashPix Image (FPX)

Figure 3 File formats

JPEG format is the most suitable format for full-colour photographs or greyscale images, such as scanned photographs, with large variations in the colour. It is not so effective for text, cartoons or black and white line drawings.

The maximum number of colours a *GIF format* image supports is 256, much less than the TIFF and JPEG formats. However, GIF format is significantly better for images with a just a few distinct colours, where the image has sharp contrasts – such as black next to white, as in cartoons.

PNG (Portable Network Graphics) is an alternative format for a variety of applications. PNG offers many of the advantages of both TIFF and GIF file formats, but the file size is smaller. This may be an important consideration, as your complete e-portfolio will be limited to a maximum file size.

Each project brief for your e-portfolio will specify acceptable file formats. These are likely to be PDF for paper-based publications, JPG or PNG for images, HTML for on-screen publications and SWF

(Flash movie) for presentations, although this may change depending on future developments. To convert files such as Word to PDF format, you will require software such as Adobe Acrobat. Files that have not been created in HTML (or web format), can be converted from Word, Excel and PowerPoint by selecting **File**, **Save As** and choosing the **Web Page** format from the *Save as type* box. You can choose other alternative formats through this method and may need to experiment to find the most suitable one.

Figure 4 Saving a Word document as a web page

Setting up folders to organise files

If you save all your files in one place on a hard drive, it can be quite difficult to find the one you want. The solution is to create a main folder for a particular project, and then sub-folders to contain particular elements of the project. Figure 5 shows a main folder called 'Digital Applications', which contains a sub-folder called 'Standard Ways'. All the work for this book was saved in the main folder, and the material for this chapter was saved in the first-level sub-folder. As more and more chapters were written, more sub-folders were created to contain them. One sub-sub-folder is called 'Screen dumps', where all the screen shots were saved in TIFF format.

If you need to copy or delete files or folders, open Explorer as explained below, right-click on the relevant file or folder and select **Copy** or **Delete**. If you are copying the file or folder, move your mouse pointer to where you wish to place the copy, right-click the mouse and select **Paste**.

Figure 5 Folders and sub-folders

Go out and try!

1 To make sure you are organised right from the start, create
   the following folders and sub-folders to save the work you
   will produce for these chapters:

      Standard Ways
      ICT Skills
         Word-processing software
         Spreadsheet software
         Presentation software
         Artwork and imaging software
         Internet and intranets
         Email
         Website software
         Collaborative software
         Project planning software
      Creating an e-portfolio
      Project Planning
      Review and Evaluation

   ○ From the **Start** menu, right-click the mouse and select
     Explore.
   ○ In the left-hand pane, click on the drive where you want
     to create your folders.
   ○ The contents of the drive are shown in the right-hand
     pane. Right-click in the white space of this section. The
     following menu appears.

TiP

*Organising your electronic
files may vary, depending on
the software available to you.*

Figure 6 Creating a new folder

   ○ Select **New** and then **Folder**. The new folder appears.
   ○ Type in the name for the folder and press **Enter**.
   ○ Repeat these steps for each of the folders and sub-folders.

Limiting access to confidential or sensitive files

Most files saved on home computers are not particularly confidential or sensitive, but business data held on a computer can often be very confidential or sensitive. For example, medical records should not be accessible to the cleaning staff in a doctor's office or a hospital. Sometimes files in business may be confidential because the company is developing a new product and does not wish its competitors to know its plans.

There are several ways to protect confidentiality.

Using an ID and password to access the computer

Business systems are usually protected by passwords. Users should be prompted to change their passwords regularly. You will notice that when you enter the password, it is displayed as a series of asterisks (**************). This is to hide the characters and prevent anyone reading your password as it is shown on the screen.

Using a password to view data

Modern software systems also allow the use of passwords when saving files. You can set a password to open the file, or a password to modify it. Some people will be able to open the file to *read* it, but they will not be allowed to make any changes.

Many organisations *rank* data files according to their degree of confidentiality. Staff can be given different security levels or privileges which limit access to only *some files* or *some fields* within a file. This is a common method of protecting data and maintaining confidentiality.

Using additional security measures

Internet banking uses a series of security methods to ensure that customers' banking details are kept safe from unauthorised access. Apart from the usual login ID and password, the customer might have to choose another password or some memorable data. This time only certain characters are entered, changing each time the customer accesses the account. This helps to protect against *key loggers*.

For example, suppose the extra password is 'England'. You will see from Figure 7 that on this occasion only the first, fourth and fifth letters of the password are requested from the customer.

Jargon buster

A **key logger** is a piece of software, installed without the user's knowledge, that records keypresses to try to find passwords.

Figure 7 Memorable data to protect confidentiality when using Internet banking

Another security measure is to limit the time that the file or web page can stay open for if it is not used. This ensures that the user's details are not left open on the computer if he or she forgets to close the file. A timeout message will appear (Figure 8).

Figure 8 A time-out warning

Using effective virus protection

A computer virus is a small program that has been developed by someone either for general mischief or to attack a particular organisation. The virus copies itself without the user intending it to, or even being aware of it happening until something goes wrong. Sometimes, in an attempt to prevent detection, the program will mutate (change) slightly each time it is copied.

Viruses can be spread by

- downloading software from the Internet
- opening an attachment to an email
- transferring files from one computer to another via a floppy disk
- using pirated software that is infected.

Your computer system is far less likely to be at risk if you

- use floppy disks only on one system
- delete emails from unknown sources, especially if they have an attachment
- regularly update your virus protection software.

Viruses can spread very quickly via email. A virus may cause problems such as clearing screens, deleting data or even making the

TiP

Make sure you run the anti-virus software at least once a week or set it to scan automatically.

TiP

It is essential to ensure that the virus definitions are kept up-to-date. Many anti-virus programs will remind you when this is necessary.

whole computer unusable. Organisations treat the risk of infection very seriously, controlling emails and not allowing staff to take disks between work and home. Anti-virus software is therefore essential, both in business and for the home user.

Anti-virus software

Anti-virus software works by scanning files to discover and remove viruses, a process known as *disinfecting*. There are thousands of viruses waiting to attack your computer. More viruses are being written all the time, so it is essential to keep your anti-virus software up to date. As soon as a new virus appears, the anti-virus companies work to produce a *pattern* file, which tells the software how to discover and stop the virus. Symantec (Norton), McAfee, Dr Solomon's and Panda are some of the companies providing anti-virus software.

Using Readme files

Readme files are files on a CD that give an explanation about how to use the software on that CD. For example, the Readme file might

- explain how to install the software
- describe important points
- give specific information that might apply to your particular setup
- say how much hard disk space is needed to install and run the software effectively
- contain late-breaking information that reveals how reported problems with the software can be solved
- link to additional resources.

Personal effectiveness

To ensure your own personal effectiveness in preparing your project, you must

- select appropriate tools and techniques
- customise settings
- create and use shortcuts
- use available sources of help
- use a plan to organise your work and meet deadlines.

We will look at each of these skills in turn.

TiP

Before you decide how to present the summative project for your e-portfolio, it is very important to think about the tools that are available to you.

Selecting appropriate tools and techniques

If you decide to use video editing in your project, but have access to a video camera and the video editing software for only one hour a week, you are not likely to be able to finish the project. Although it might be a very interesting, exciting project about which you are really enthusiastic, if you can't resolve the problem of access to the equipment it is better to think again and choose an alternative project or presentation style.

Once you have decided on the tools to use, you should then think about suitable, effective techniques that you could apply. For example, if you are fortunate enough to have a video camera and video editing software available, you may need advice on the best techniques to use when making the film. No matter how great your expertise in editing the film, if the original material is poor because there has been too much zooming in and out, and the sweeps across the views were too fast, then the end product is unlikely to be successful.

Customising settings

You can use the Control Panel to personalise your computer in numerous ways, for example by

- changing the appearance and colour scheme of your screen
- choosing a screen saver
- selecting the date, time and language settings
- changing the mouse buttons for a left-handed person.

Software applications, such as Word, Excel and Access, come with default settings pre-installed during manufacture, but there are many ways to customise the settings to suit your needs. For example, you would probably find the *Standard*, *Formatting* and possibly *Drawing* toolbars to be visible. As you can see from Figure 9, in Word there are 16 toolbars in total – but if most or all of them were shown at once, the screen would be far too cluttered, with not much room left for the page you were working on! Instead,

Figure 9 Toolbars available in Word

(a)

Microsoft
Outlook

Microsoft
Access

Microsoft
Publisher

Microsoft Excel

Microsoft Word

POWERPNT

(b)

Shortcut to
Digital
Applications

Figure 10 (a) Shortcuts on the desktop to software installed on the computer. (b) A shortcut to files for this book

select the ones most useful to you. Word is often set with a default font of Times New Roman 10pt, which is too small for everyday use, so you might wish to set the default to a different size and style.

Creating and using shortcuts

Every time you click on an icon on a toolbar – such as save 💾 or print 🖨 – you are using a *shortcut*. Using the print icon allows you to print the document in a single step. If you use **File**, **Print** and **OK** it is at least three steps – but you might want to choose this method if you want to print two or more copies, or only certain pages.

Each of the toolbars has a list of shortcut icons, but only those most frequently used are automatically visible. You can choose to add any others that you find useful. For example, if you frequently send documents as attachments to an email, you might wish to add the relevant icon 📎 to the toolbar.

Shortcuts can also be placed on the desktop. No doubt you are familiar with using shortcuts to software applications – see Figure 10(a). However, you can also choose to create shortcuts to files or folders that you use regularly. For example, a shortcut to the folder containing your work for this qualification might prove useful – see Figure 10(b).

Getting help

There will be a variety of sources of help available to you, and it is a good idea to take advantage of them. You may find help through

- software help files
- textbooks
- your teacher
- specialist staff within your school or college

- your peers (who may be more knowledgeable about some aspects of the software, whereas you may know more about other aspects and can offer them help in return)
- family or friends who are experienced in the project you are undertaking.

Using a plan to organise work and meet deadlines

In order to complete your e-portfolio you will have to undertake a number of tasks, gradually building up the content. All the various sections of the e-portfolio will need to be completed to a deadline.

When the final deadline is a long time ahead, it is all too easy to keep thinking there is no rush, and then find you are trying to do ten things at once and cannot possibly finish everything in time! Therefore it is essential to think about all the various items that will go into the e-portfolio and then plan a schedule of your work.

Remember that *it always takes longer than you think*, so make sure you plan to finish well before the final deadline, to allow for all those unexpected delays!

Skills check ▷▷

Information on how to plan and organise your work is presented in more detail in the chapter on project planning (page 199).

Quality assurance

To ensure that your work is accurate and effective, you will need to
- use tools such as spelling and grammar checks, and Print Preview
- proofread your work
- seek the views of others
- check your research.

Using spelling and grammar checks and Print Preview

Spellcheckers

TiP

Be aware that many computer programs use American spellings of words. These are often slightly different from the British spellings.

Spelling errors spoil your work, so always use a *spellchecker* to detect words spelt incorrectly and repeated words (for example, 'and and'). Spellcheckers are available not only in word processors, but also in most other applications such as spreadsheets and email programs. Spellcheckers compare the words you have written against a list in the computer's dictionary, then any words not matching are queried and possible alternatives are suggested.

Figure 11 Adding a word to the spellchecker dictionary

But beware! Although the spellchecker is an excellent tool, it does not understand what you are trying to say and so it can be wrong. This means that *it is still important for the operator to have a reasonable level of spelling!* For example, it will not correct 'whether' for 'weather', or 'to', 'too' or 'two' used in the wrong place.

Sometimes a spellchecker will suggest that a word is incorrect when you know that it is correct. The dictionary will include common names such as 'Smith' but not unusual names such as 'Tenterden', which is a village in Kent. For this the dictionary suggested three alternatives (Figure 11), but the name was spelt correctly.

If you are likely to use a particular word frequently, then it is worth adding it to the dictionary. You can right-click on the word and select the **Add** option. In future the spelling checker will accept the word.

Sometimes words are indicated as incorrect because the language of the spellchecker is set to English (US) not English (UK), so it's worth checking. Select **Tools, Language, Set Language** and choose **English (UK)** and **Default** (Figure 12).

Figure 12 Setting the language that Word will use for its spellchecker

Grammar checker

The *grammar checker* can be more complicated and difficult to use than a spellchecker, and therefore tends to be rather less popular. As a starting point, the best way to use a basic grammar checker is as a tool to draw your attention to possible mistakes. It can be very useful for finding typing errors; such as the one shown in Figure 13, where

Figure 13 The grammar checker showing that there is no space after the bracket

there is no space after the closing bracket. At other times the suggestions may not be clear, so *think about* the suggestions made – the final decision is yours.

Print Preview

Before sending your work to the printer, it is a good idea to check it in Print Preview, where you will often identify poor layout that can be corrected before printing. This saves time and prevents you wasting paper.

When the author of this chapter used Print Preview at this point, it revealed a blank page that hadn't been noticed, which would have interfered with page numbering. It was an easy matter to delete the page before printing the file.

Proofreading your work

Even though you read your work on the monitor screen, it is surprising how often errors can be missed that the spelling or grammar checks have not shown up. In addition, you often find that although you were clear in your mind what you wanted to say, on re-reading the text you realise it is muddled, or you haven't fully explained the topic.

As authors of this book we received the proofs (the first copy of the book as it would look when finally printed) and we had to check that everything was correct, including the page layouts. At this stage we made some changes to our original work, not because it was necessarily wrong, but because it wasn't as clear as we wanted it, or it needed to be a little more detailed.

Seeking the views of others

Once you have an idea about the project you wish to undertake, it is excellent practice to ask other people what they think of the idea.

When writing this book, we discussed the syllabus and decided which of us was going to undertake which sections. We also brainstormed ideas about what should be included, and the presentation. Each one of us came up with ideas and suggestions, and together we produced (we hope!) a better result than if we had worked separately.

We also read each other's material and often asked colleagues to read what we had written. As an author you can be 'too close' to your own project to spot minor errors, whereas someone independent

TiP

If your work is web-based, make sure you check it using different browser software on several computers. Is it always displayed as you had intended?

TiP

Proofreading isn't the most popular task, but it is important. You might discover silly errors, or an explanation that doesn't quite say what you intended. Correcting it before handing in your assignment or course-work might make all the difference to your final grade.

TiP

Do ask someone else's opinion of the work you have produced for your e-portfolio – and do take note of the comments made. A critical evaluation of your project should be viewed as helpful advice to enable you to improve what you have done, not as a negative criticism.

notices odd little mistakes, or a paragraph that is not clear. These can be edited to improve the final version. It is very important to keep draft versions of your work so you can show changes made as a result of comments from others.

Authenticating your work – checking your research

In general, textbooks are likely to contain reliable information because they will have been written to provide students with the information they need for a course they are studying, and are published by reputable companies. If it became obvious that an author or publisher was producing unreliable textbooks, they would soon go out of business: no one would buy their books.

Probably, by the time you read this book, information such as the amount of data a memory stick can hold will have changed. This does not mean that it contains deliberate misinformation – it's just that technology advances. If you do make use of that kind of data given in a book then it would be wise to check whether it is still accurate.

Figure 14 Discussing your work with other people

As you are well aware, the Internet is an amazing tool to use when researching almost any topic you could think of. It is, however, all too easy to drop into the trap of *believing everything on the Internet is accurate and reliable*. Unfortunately, that is not the case. Anyone can set up a website and put information on that site. Sometimes the author genuinely believes that the information posted is authentic or accurate, but sometimes the author wishes to deliberately mislead. Therefore, when using websites to obtain information, it is very important to use sites – such as those of the BBC or other well-known organisations – where it is likely that information given will be authentic.

✓ TiP

*In order to authenticate your own work, try researching through **a variety of sources**. If they all match each other, then you can be confident that the information you have obtained is accurate and reliable.*

Legislation and codes of practice

To ensure that you comply with legislation and codes of practice relating to the use of ICT, you will need to

- acknowledge your sources
- avoid plagiarism
- respect copyright
- protect confidentiality.

Acknowledging your sources and avoiding plagiarism

In order to complete your portfolio evidence you will need to undertake research. This may be from books, from newspapers or journals, from the Internet, or from people through surveys, questionnaires or face-to-face discussions. It is essential that you acknowledge where you obtained this information – your *sources*.

In some cases you may have to gain permission from the author, artist or relevant organisation to use the material. You should also include a *bibliography* of books, journals, articles and websites that you have found useful in your research.

People may copy original work and present it as their own. This is much easier to do from ICT systems (and especially from the Internet) than it is from a paper-based source such as a textbook. This is called *plagiarism* and, because it breaks copyright law (explained opposite), it is a serious offence.

It is quite acceptable to *quote* a reasonable amount of someone else's work, as long as you put inverted commas (" ") at the beginning of the text and at the end, and identify the original author, the book, web address or newspaper where you found the information.

Jargon buster

A **bibliography** is a list of sources of information that were useful when undertaking your research, and helped you to form your own opinions when writing an essay or producing the e-portfolio. For example, if you have a project to design a website, you might study other websites first to help you decide what makes an effective site and what doesn't.

The bibliography should include enough information for other people to be able to find the same source you used: the book, journal or newspaper, title of the article, author, date of publication, and web address.

Assessment Hint

*Note that your portfolio evidence will **not** be acceptable if it is a succession of quotes from other people, with very little original effort on your part.*

 Think it over...

Check out the sources that we might have used when writing this textbook.

Respecting copyright

You are probably familiar with *copyright* warnings at the beginning of books, rental videos and DVDs, when there is a statement along the lines of *'All rights reserved. No part of this publication may be reproduced or transmitted, in any form or by any means, without the prior permission of the publisher.'* This is also true for most computer programs, published text and images.

Check for the symbol ©, followed by a date and sometimes a name, as shown at the beginning of this book. This indicates that the work is covered by copyright. It is very important to understand what copyright means and to respect copyright law (Figure 15).

- The Copyright Designs and Patents Act 1988 was originally set up in order to protect the work of authors, artists and composers from being reproduced or copied without permission.

- Current European copyright law extends for 70 years after the death of the author/creator. During this period, the work (book, work of art, software, photograph, music score, etc.) may not be reproduced without permission.

- This original Copyright Designs and Patents Act was in existence long before computers were invented. It has subsequently been extended to include computer software, making it illegal to copy applications without permission from the copyright holder.

Figure 15 Facts about the Copyright Designs and Patents Act

When you buy computer software it generally comes with a *licence* that allows you to install, use, access, display or run just one copy of the software on one computer and one notebook. Your school or college will have purchased a network licence in order to be granted permission to run the software on all of its machines.

Imagine a small business that started with just one computer. The owner bought the software for that computer and will have the necessary licence. As the business expands, he might decide to install a network and use the same software on the network, forgetting to buy a new licence. He has in fact broken the law, even though it was not intentional.

This law affects everyone who owns a computer. You must not let other people borrow your software to install on their computers. Similarly, you should not borrow software from a friend and install it on your computer. The software houses have, after all, invested a great deal of time and money in order to develop the software, so you are stealing from them by not paying for the software. It's no different from going into a shop and stealing a box of chocolates or a DVD.

In order to help protect software copyright, the Federation Against Software Theft (FAST) was set up in 1984 to investigate software piracy. The federation will prosecute when instances of illegal copying of software come to their attention. Be warned!

Protecting confidentiality

The Data Protection Act of 1994, which was updated in 1998, was introduced to deal with the increasing amount of personal data being held on computers and the potential misuse of that personal data. Think of the many different organisations that hold computerised records containing details of our personal lives, school records, employment history, financial and medical records, criminal activities, etc. Under the Data Protection Act, these organisations must ensure that the data remains confidential. They must also allow people to access the data that is being held about them, in return for a small administration fee.

Both employers and employees have a responsibility under the Act to ensure that personal information is not disclosed, however innocently. Staff must be aware of straightforward things they can do to protect the confidentiality of the data. Examples are described in Figure 16.

Apart from personal information, a commercial organisation will want to keep information about the company confidential. They do

- Passwords should be kept secret. A note stuck to the side of your computer is not a sensible way to remember your password!

- Personal information should not be passed on to third parties at any time. Imagine a situation where an insurance company employee had access to personal information. Think of the consequences if a list of addresses and details of valuable house contents fell into the wrong hands.

- Staff working with confidential data must be very careful not to disclose personal information during a conversation, however innocently.

- Computer screens in public places – such as a doctor's surgery – should not be visible to the general public. It could be very unfortunate if somebody waiting at the reception desk read personal and confidential information about another patient.

Figure 16 Facts about passwords

Skills check ⟩⟩

The information on confidential or sensitive files on page 68 is also relevant here.

not want their competitors finding out how well or badly they are doing, and what new products or designs are being prepared.

Organisations have always been at risk from dishonest staff, but the main difference since the arrival of computers is that it is so much easier to obtain the information – you do not even need to be in the room or the building! Inevitably there has to be trust in and reliance on the users of ICT, especially in a business environment. In fact most people are honest and have no intention of defrauding their employer or disclosing confidential information.

It is essential to take security issues seriously, so that you do not *unintentionally* give someone else access to uncensored or private materials. Also, if you *accidentally* discover uncensored or private materials, you must not take advantage of the opportunity, and it may be appropriate to report that a breach of security has occurred.

Naturally we all chat about our jobs, but it is important to know which information should be kept to ourselves, and when it is OK to talk about something to a friend or relative. If in doubt then keep quiet.

Working safely

Employers are responsible for promoting health and safety in the workplace. However, each employee also has the duty to take sensible precautions. For example, if you spend a lot of time using a computer, you may tend to develop backache, eyestrain or repetitive strain injury, but good working practices will greatly reduce the risk of suffering from such problems. It is important to

- ensure that the positioning of hardware, cables and seating is correct
- check that the lighting is appropriate
- take regular breaks
- handle and store media correctly.

Positioning hardware, cables and seating

Desks should have a non-reflective surface and be at the correct height with sufficient space for a computer, mouse mat, telephone and supporting documents. There should be enough space around the desk for you to change position and vary your movements. It may be beneficial to use a wrist rest to support your wrists.

The ideal working position is to sit with your eyes level with the top of the screen, the small of your back against the chair, and your feet flat on the floor (Figure 17).

Since we all come in different shapes and sizes, it is important to use a chair that can be adjusted to suit the user. A good computer chair will have five feet with castors to increase stability and to allow freedom of movement. You will be able to adjust the height of the seat to suit your own height, as well as the position and tilt of the backrest in order to support your back. If you are short and your feet don't reach the floor, you can ask for a footrest to be provided so that you can support your feet and legs.

Cables should be correctly and safely positioned where no one can fall or trip over them. They should be securely fastened, usually inside trunking that is attached to the walls. They should *never* be trailing across the floor.

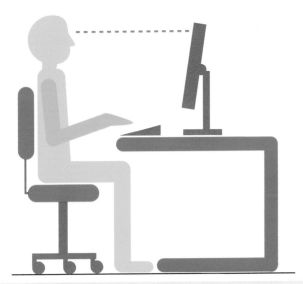

Figure 17 The fundamentals of good posture at a computer workstation

Using appropriate lighting

The ideal position for the computer monitor is at right-angles to a window. In order to keep sun off the screen and help reduce glare, blinds should be provided at the windows. If glare is a problem then an anti-glare shield can be fitted. The office should be well lit and the lighting should offer a contrast between the screen and surrounding area. If the light is too dim, documents will be hard to read, leading to eyestrain. If necessary, adjust the brightness of the screen in response to changes in light.

Taking regular breaks

Bad posture is the main cause of backache. If you work *continuously* at a computer monitor you should be allowed to take a short break (say 5–10 minutes) away from the screen after an hour's *uninterrupted* screen or keyboard work. Ideally your job will involve a variety of tasks so that this situation will not arise in the first place.

Handling and storing media correctly

It is important to know how to protect the media you are using, by handling and storing them correctly. Care should be taken when handling floppy disks, CDs and DVDs in order to protect the data. Store them in protective cases to keep them clean, away from dust and moisture. Avoid touching the surfaces, and keep them away from extremes of temperature.

? Think it over ...

How safe is your working environment at home? What could you change to improve it?

Section 2 ICT skills

Word-processing software

If somebody asked you 'What is word-processing?' you would probably describe it as *the process of creating, storing and editing text-based documents*. While you would be quite right in saying this, in fact word-processing offers so much more.

Word-processing is one of the most effective ways of communicating information to other people through paper-based documents such as letters, reports, leaflets, newsletters, posters and flyers. In fact, effective word-processing skills also underlie successful communication through on-screen publications such as presentations or web pages.

Your word-processing skills are a valuable asset that you will make use of throughout your student and adult life. Word-processing is more than just sitting down at a computer and producing a document without a second thought. It is the skill of designing a document to convey specific information to different groups of people.

LEARNING OUTCOMES

You need to learn about
✓ entering, cutting, copying, pasting and moving text
✓ formatting text
✓ using paragraph formatting features
✓ using page formatting features
✓ using tables
✓ creating, selecting and inserting components
✓ using images/objects
✓ using spelling and grammar checkers
✓ using mail merge.

Entering, cutting, copying, pasting and moving text

Entering text

Text is keyed in (or *entered*) via the keyboard. When a word will not fit on the end of a line, it is moved on to the next line. This feature is called *word wrap,* and the word processor automatically inserts *soft returns* at the end of each line. These soft returns are adjustable and will move within the document if necessary – such as when you insert an extra word or two in a paragraph or decide to delete some text.

You only need to use the **Enter** key when you want to start a new line, perhaps after a heading or at the start of a new paragraph. The returns that *you* put into a document are called *hard returns* and they are not adjustable by the software. If you display the formatting marks in a document by selecting the **Show/Hide** icon on the *Standard* toolbar, the ¶ character identifies all hard returns.

As you enter text, there are some basic steps you can take to improve the general presentation of the document:

- For most text-based documents, a font size of 11pt or 12pt will be appropriate.
- Remember to leave one clear line space (achieved by pressing the **Enter** key twice) after a heading and between each paragraph. Look at Figure 18, where the ¶ symbol shows that the **Enter** key has been used.
- Nowadays it is common practice when using a word processor to leave only one space following a sentence. However, in the days of the typewriter, it was standard practice to leave two spaces following any punctuation at the end of a sentence. There are many people today who feel that using two spaces between sentences makes your text easier to read because the sentences stand out clearly. You must make your own decision or follow the guidance from your teacher/tutor.
- Leave one space after all other punctuation.
- If possible, use a *fully blocked* style of presentation when producing letters, reports, etc. This means that everything starts at the left-hand margin. Figure 18 is an example of fully blocked working.

Jargon buster

A manual typewriter has a **carriage return key**, which the typist must press between lines to return the carriage to the left of the paper. Because of this the **Enter** key is sometimes called the **Return** key, and the hidden characters it inserts into documents are called **returns**.

Skills check ▷▷

Refer to page 86 for more detailed information on font sizes.

TiP

You can use styles (see page 102) to add space after headings and between paragraphs automatically.

```
Travelbug¶
¶
17·London·Road¶
Whychton¶
TO9·3WN¶
¶
Tel: → 543·2134·5678¶
Fax: → 543·2134·5679¶
Email:·travelbug@userve.co.uk¶
¶
¶
¶
There·is·so·much·to·see·and·do·in·Brussels·that·a·weekend·just·won't·be·long·enough!¶
¶
There·are·over·30·museums·to·visit,·fine·restaurants·and·bars,·shops·selling·anything·
from·high·fashion·to·antiques·to·sophisticated·chocolate·creations.··Browse·the·open-
air·markets·or·stroll·around·the·magnificent·cobbled·Grand·Place.¶
¶
A·visit·to·Brussels·isn't·complete·without·a·visit·to·the·famous·Manneken·Pis,·which·
can·be·guaranteed·to·draw·a·crowd.¶
¶
Travel·by·Eurostar·from·Waterloo·and·arrive·in·Brussels·in·2·hours·20·minutes.··
Selected·services·also·available·from·Ashford·International·Station·in·Kent.¶
¶
Prices·start·at·£125.00·for·2·nights.¶
¶
```

Figure 18 An example of work presented in a 'fully blocked' style

Cut, copy, move and paste

A significant benefit of word processors is that they let you cut, copy, move and paste text. These features allow you to edit (change) the on-screen text without having to retype the whole document.

It is easy to get muddled over the meaning of the terms *cut*, *copy*, *move* and *paste*.

- **Cut** ✂ deletes the selected text and places a copy onto the *Clipboard* (a special part of the computer's memory) from where it can be retrieved.

- **Copy** 📄 copies the selected text onto the Clipboard, without deleting it. It can then be placed elsewhere in the document.

- **Move** means to cut selected text from one place and immediately paste that text elsewhere in the document.

- **Paste** 📋 inserts the text from the Clipboard elsewhere in the document, or even into a different document.

Formatting text

Font type and font size

A *font* is the name given to describe the style of typeface you are using. Two popular styles frequently used in the preparation of business documents are Times New Roman and Arial.

- This is an example of Times New Roman. It is referred to as a *serif* font because of the 'little feet' at the bottom of each letter.
- This is an example of Arial. It is referred to as a *sans serif* font because it does not have the 'little feet'.

Your default font will generally be Times New Roman, and the size is likely to be somewhere between 10 and 12 points. *Point* refers to the size of the character – the higher the number, the larger the font. A point size of 72 would give you a letter approximately 2.54 cm (1 inch) tall.

It is important that you choose a style and size of font to suit the task you are doing. Some font styles are rather elaborate and difficult to read, so you should use them with care. Similarly, choose a suitable font size.

For example, text contained in a poster will probably need to be quite large so that it is eye-catching and can be read from a distance. In contrast, a leaflet or newsletter might contain fairly large headings, with the body text printed in a smaller font.

TiP

Most business documents will rely on the use of capital letters, bold, underline or italic to emphasise any key points to be made.

Bold, underline and italic

In addition to using different font styles and sizes, you can also use **bold,** <u>underline</u> or *italic* to emphasise text. ***<u>However, it is not generally a good idea to apply all three to the same text!</u>***

Using colour

Colour is not generally applied to text in standard documents, such as letters or reports, but it can be very effective in leaflets, posters, flyers, etc. However, for it to be effective you should use it in moderation – otherwise your document will be messy, difficult to read and therefore may not be fit for the purpose intended.

Your word-processing software has a selection of standard colours (Figure 19(a)). It also has the facility to customise a colour

(Figure 19(b)), which can be useful if you need to match an existing colour. For example, some companies have 'corporate colours' that they replicate on their logo, advertising material, brochures, on-screen presentations, and so on.

(a)

(b)

Figure 19 (a) The standard colour palette and (b) the custom colour option

Using paragraph formatting features

Alignment

Usually your text automatically lines up against the left-hand margin, leaving the right-hand margin uneven (or *ragged*). This is because the default style of paragraph alignment is *left aligned*. Word-processing software offers you alternative styles of paragraph format, such as *justified* or *centred*.

Here the text is **left-aligned** and the right-hand margin is uneven or *ragged*. This is the default setting. The spaces between words are equal.	Here the alignment is **justified** and both the left and right margins are straight. The program automatically adjusts the spaces between words to distribute the text evenly between the margins. The spaces between words are not equal.	Here the text is **centred** between the margins. This is generally used for presentation and display rather than letters or notes.

Figure 20 Text left-aligned, justified and centred

The default setting of left alignment is quite acceptable for most text-based documents and on-screen presentations. However, there are occasions when justified alignment may be more appropriate. For example, a newsletter produced in columns looks more professional with justified margins (Figure 21(a)). Lines of text in a poster may be centred between the margins; in order to balance the presentation, paragraphs in the same poster look neater if they are justified, leaving an equal space against the left and the right margins (Figure 21(b)).

Bullets and numbering

Bullet points are used to make items in a list stand out. The standard bullet point is represented by the character symbol ●, but you can choose different symbols. For example

- a bullet point chosen from the standard selection in Bullets and Numbering
- a bullet point customised from a selection in Wingdings
- a bullet point customised from a selection in Webdings.

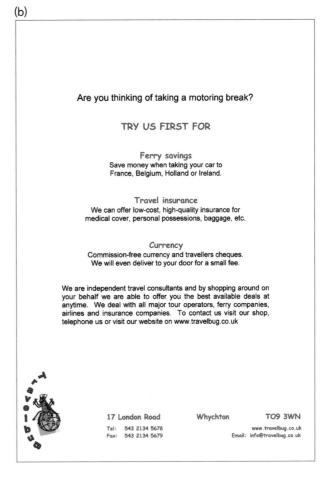

(a)

TRAVELBUG NEWSFLASH

Issue No 1   September 2005

Save £££s on your next ferry crossing

Whether you are going across the channel as part of your holiday or popping over to France to re-stock the wine rack, take advantage of great savings of up to 15%.

Cruise Club

Our Cruise Club is free to join and you will receive regular information about the latest cruise news together with special offers from all major cruise lines. Book online and get an extra 5% discount!

Travel Insurance

Every year hundreds of thousands of Britons on holiday abroad need medical treatment, lose their baggage or have their holidays cancelled. Our special travel insurance covers you for medical treatment, luggage and holiday cancellation. We guarantee that our rates for comprehensive insurance are cheaper than all major insurance companies.

Ski deals

Fully inclusive hotel and chalet holidays in Europe and USA. We specialise in group travel and can offer exciting deals for parties of 10 or more.

UK short breaks

Up to 15% off short breaks with the Merit Hotel Group. Their 4-star and 5-star hotels offer swimming pools, beauty spas and award winning restaurants in 35 major UK cities. An additional 20 country hotels have 18-hole golf courses and can arrange other activities such as horse riding and water sports.

Flights

We deal with all major airlines, including low cost operators, and can guarantee the cheapest prices available. Book early for the best deals. Airport car parking can also be arranged.

Currency

Commission free currency and travellers cheques available over the counter for personal callers. Telephone by 1500 hours and we will guarantee delivery to your door the following day for a small fee (minimum order applies). Visit our website for more information.

Holiday bookings

Save a minimum of 5% on a large range of holidays to Europe, USA, Canada and Australia. Full details available on our website.

17 London Road   Whychton   TO9 3WN

Tel: 543 2134 5678   www.travelbug.co.uk
Fax: 543 2134 5679   Email: info@travelbug.co.uk

(b)

Are you thinking of taking a motoring break?

TRY US FIRST FOR

Ferry savings
Save money when taking your car to
France, Belgium, Holland or Ireland.

Travel insurance
We can offer low-cost, high-quality insurance for
medical cover, personal possessions, baggage, etc.

Currency
Commission-free currency and travellers cheques.
We will even deliver to your door for a small fee.

We are independent travel consultants and by shopping around on your behalf we are able to offer you the best available deals at anytime. We deal with all major tour operators, ferry companies, airlines and insurance companies. To contact us visit our shop, telephone us or visit our website on www.travelbug.co.uk

17 London Road   Whychton   TO9 3WN

Tel: 543 2134 5678   www.travelbug.co.uk
Fax: 543 2134 5679   Email: info@travelbug.co.uk

Figure 21 (a) A newsletter and (b) a poster

As you can see from these examples, the standard bullet point is the clearest and is the style most commonly used in the preparation of paper-based documents.

Sometimes different styles of bullet point are used to indicate different 'levels' in a list. For example:

- Fully-inclusive holidays
  - » Full-board
  - » Half-board
  - » Self-catering
- Activity holidays
  - » Skiing
  - » Water sports

The important thing to remember is that you should use a style of bullet that is fit for the purpose of the document. Use the decorative or picture bullets only for more informal documents, on-screen presentations or web pages.

Sometimes it is preferable to number a list rather than using bullets. Most word processors offer a variety of options – such as **1, 2, 3** or **a), b), c)**. Figure 22 shows both bullets and numbering used in a document.

TRAVELBUG CRUISE CLUB

Our Cruise Club is totally independent and we can therefore offer a varied range of cruises from all leading cruise line operators. Our knowledgeable staff are on hand 7 days a week to help you plan the perfect trip.

Membership is free and Cruise Club members have the following advantages:

- 2 for 1 cruise offers
- Services of our specially trained staff
- Monthly newsletter with the latest information and offers
- Cabin upgrades and on-ship spending vouchers
- Exclusive visits to see the ships whilst docked in the UK
- Specially discounted rates

How to join

1. Call us for an application form or download from our web site
2. Complete the application form
3. Return to us in Whychton
4. Your application membership pack will be sent out by return post.

Figure 22 The use of bullet points and numbering

Tabs

The **Tab** key is located to the left of the letter Q on your keyboard. Every time you press the **Tab** key the cursor jumps across the page. The **Tab** key is used to place and align text on the page.

In the example in Figure 23, tabs have been used to position the three columns headed 'Coffee', 'Beer' and 'Meal for 2 people'.

Approximate costs						
→	→	Coffee	→	Beer→	→	Meal for 2 people
France→	→	£1.40→	→	£2.50→	→	£44.00
Italy→	→	£0.70→	→	£1.45→	→	£27.50
Spain→	→	£0.80→	→	£1.00→	→	£20.00

Figure 23 The use of tabs to form a simple table

Figure 24 illustrates Microsoft Word's ruler. If you look closely you will see very feint vertical marks along the bottom edge.

These marks represent the default tabulation settings (or tab settings) and are positioned at 1.27-cm ($\frac{1}{2}$-inch) intervals.

Figure 24 The ruler and default tab settings

Tab styles

The default tab settings are known as *left tabs* because the text is left-aligned with the tab. There are three other useful tab settings illustrated in Figure 25:

- right – text is right-aligned with the tab
- centre – text extends either side of the tab setting
- decimal – text before the decimal point extends left and after the decimal point extends right.

4 STAR OFFERS

Date	Place	Hotel	No. of Nights	Cost
10 October	Derby	Broadmeadow	4	£210
16 November	Chester	Lodge Gate	6	£249.50
23 November	Edinburgh	Monterry	5	£265.99
6 December	Brighton	Hurlingham Park	1	£75
13 December	London	Stretford	2	£150
↑ Left		↑ Right	↑ Centred	↑ Decimal

Figure 25 Column alignments in a tabbed table

Indents

Paragraph indents can be used to make paragraphs stand out. Indents can be applied by selecting **Format, Paragraph** from the menu, or by dragging the indent markers on the horizontal ruler (Figure 26). Figure 27 shows some examples of paragraph indents in a newsletter.

← First line indent
← Hanging indent

Figure 26 Indent markers on the horizontal ruler

TRAVELBUG CITY BREAKS

Luxury coach tours
5 nights from £139.00
Nationwide pick-up points

Take advantage of the special deals we have negotiated with Whychton Coach Company and travel to one of your favourite European destinations by luxury, air-conditioned coach. All coaches have facilities for refreshments, WCs and videos and for your safety 2 qualified coach drivers accompany all journeys.

Paris is a shopper's paradise and is renowned as a city of culture. Your first stop must be the Louvre to see the Mona Lisa and Pei's glass pyramid. If Art Nouveau and Impressionism are more to your liking, then a visit to the Musée d'Orsay is a must.

Barcelona is the place to go to see the unmistakable works of Gaudi. Visit his distinctive houses in the Paseo de Gracia or the awe-inspiring church of the Sagrada Familia. Stroll through Las Ramblas to the busy port and Gothic Quarter.

Venice is a beautiful city and an unforgettable experience. Everybody goes about their business on the broad canals and narrow waterways. The famous Rialto Bridge is lined with shops selling glass, lace and carnival masks. St. Mark's Square is the place to be seen.

Florence represents the cultural heart of Italy and is packed with splendid architecture and fine art, including Michelangelo's famous statue of David and paintings by Raphael, Botticelli and da Vinci.

17 London Road   Whychton   TO9 3WN
Tel: 543 2134 5678   www.travelbug.co.uk
Fax: 543 2134 5679   Email: info@travelbug.co.uk

Figure 27 Examples of indents on a newsletter

Using page formatting features

Margins

The *margin* is the area around the edge of the page that generally remains free of text. The default margins leave approximately 2.54 cm (1 inch) at the top and bottom of the page, and 3.17 cm (1.25 inches) on the left and right sides (Figure 28). For most everyday word-processing tasks these margins are quite appropriate.

Sometimes, however, it is sensible to change one or more of the margin settings. If you are producing a document that is to be bound, such as a report or brochure, then a *gutter* ensures that sufficient space is left so that the binding does not block out the text.

Figure 28 An A4 page showing the margin settings

If you are creating a double-sided document, *mirror margins* ensure that the margins on the left page are a mirror image of those on the right page.

Page orientation

Most documents containing text are produced using the default page orientation of *portrait*. However, there are times when you might want or need to turn the page the other way round, to *landscape* (Figure 29).

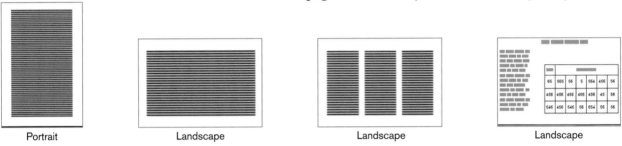

| Portrait | Landscape | Landscape | Landscape |

Figure 29 Page orientations: landscape can be very effective if you are working in columns or producing tables of data

The margin settings and page orientation (sometimes called alignment) are generally changed through **File, Page Setup**. However, dragging the left and right margin markers on the ruler is an alternative way to change margins.

Page breaks

When you are working on a long document and you run out of space on the page, the text automatically runs onto the next page. Your word-processing software has inserted a *soft page break* and forced the remaining text on to a new page. A soft page break is flexible – rather like the soft returns we looked at on page 84. If you delete a section of text in front of a soft page break, text on the following page moves up to fill the gap.

Usually when this occurs we don't have to worry about it. However, look at Figure 30. The soft page break has left the heading 'PERSONAL BAGGAGE' on one page and the paragraph that should be with it is on the following page. This is not acceptable.

In situations like this you can use a *hard* (or *manual*) *page break* to push the heading onto the next page (Figure 31). A hard page break is not flexible – it will always force a new page at the point you have inserted it, even if text is later inserted or deleted.

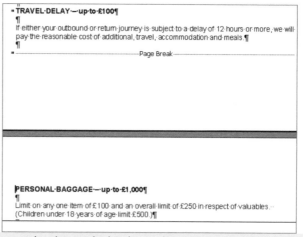

> **TRAVEL DELAY – up to £100**
>
> If either your outbound or return journey is subject to a delay of 12 hours or more, we will pay the reasonable cost of additional, travel, accommodation and meals.
>
> **PERSONAL BAGGAGE – up to £1,000**
>
>
> Limit on any one item of £100 and an overall limit of £250 in respect of valuables. (Children under 18 years of age limit £500.)
>
> **PERSONAL MONEY – up to £200**
>
> (Children under 18 years limit £50.)

Figure 30 A soft page break has been inserted by the program, but immediately under a heading

Figure 31 The user has inserted a hard page break to prevent the heading from being separated from the text beneath it (compare this with Figure 30)

There are two ways to insert a hard page break. Whichever way you choose, position the cursor immediately in front of the text that is to move onto the next page. Either

- select **Insert, Break, Page break**; or
- use key strokes – hold down **Ctrl** and at the same time press **Enter**.

By using the **Show/Hide** ¶ option you can see where the hard page break has been inserted.

Headers and footers

Anything inserted as a *header* or *footer* will appear on every page of the document in the same position (Figure 32).

Figure 32 The header and footer areas in a document

- The document *header* is the space in the top margin above the first line of text on a page. You might find a company name or the title of the document inserted in the header area.
- The document *footer* is the space at the bottom of the page after the last line of text. The date, page number and file reference are often inserted in the footer.

When you use the word processor to produce any work at school or college, it is a good idea to put your name in the header or footer. There is a selection of options available through **Insert AutoText** in the header and footer areas. From this selection you can choose to show in the header or footer a variety of information, such as filename and path. This will help you to locate a document easily at a later date. *Last printed* is also useful to check that you are looking at the most recent copy of a printed document.

Page numbers

When producing a multi-page document, it is very sensible to number the pages. Page numbers can be placed in the header or footer area of the page either through **View, Header and Footer** or through **Insert, Page Numbers**.

Line spacing

The distance between each line of text in a paragraph is known as the *line spacing*. The default setting in your word processor will produce text in single line spacing. However, there are occasions when it is useful to leave a larger space between the lines. For instance, you might want to make a section of text stand out, or to leave room between lines to make handwritten notes (Figure 33).

This example of text has been produced in **single line spacing**. This is the default setting and is probably the most commonly used.	This example shows text in **one and a half line spacing**. It is used to make sections of text stand out and therefore become easier to read.	This example shows text produced in **double line spacing**. It is particularly effective if you wish to write notes between the lines, as on a draft document.

Figure 33 Examples of single, 1.5 and double line spacings

Using columns

Word makes it easy to set up multiple columns on the same page. This is particularly useful if you are writing a newsletter.

Figure 35 Options for columns

The easy way to set up columns is to use the **Columns** icon on the *Standard* toolbar. This pops up an area that lets you choose how many columns you want (see Figure 34).

Figure 34 Setting two columns

If you need to use more advanced features, such as uneven column widths, you can select **Format, Columns** from the menu. This displays the *Columns* dialogue box shown in Figure 35.

Tables

We have already seen on page 90 that columns of data can be presented tidily by using tabs. A more powerful option, which can help you to display information effectively, is to use *tables*.

Tables consist of rows and columns that form individual boxes (or *cells*) – rather like a spreadsheet. Each individual cell may contain any amount of text, a picture or even a mathematical formula.

Figure 36 shows a basic table prepared by Travelbug to tell their customers the price of overnight accommodation in France.

Hotel stopovers
Prices shown in £s per room

Category	Accommodation	Weekend	Extra Child
Room only	Twin/double	£35	N/A
	Family	£45	2 free
Bed and Breakfast	Twin/double	£55	1 free
	Family	£75	2 free

Figure 36 A basic table layout

Borders and shading in tables

There are additional features in your word-processing software that give you the opportunity to enhance or improve the general appearance of a table. For example you can apply borders and shading, and introduce colour.

Figure 37 shows the table from Figure 36 with the addition of some features.

Hotel stopovers
Prices shown in £s per room

Category	Accommodation	Weekend	Extra Child
Room only	Twin/double	£35	N/A
	Family	£45	2 free
Bed and Breakfast	Twin/double	£55	1 free
	Family	£75	2 free

Figure 37 The table in Figure 36 with the addition of an outside border, shading and colour

Modifying row and column sizes

The columns showing prices for weekends and extra child details are wider than they need to be. The column width can be modified by picking up the arrow shape ↔ and dragging the column border to a new position. The effect of doing this is shown in Figure 38.

You can also modify the row height by picking up the arrow shape ↕ and dragging up or down.

Hotel stopovers
Prices shown in £s per room

Category	Accommodation	Weekend	Extra Child
Room only	Twin/double	£35	N/A
	Family	£45	2 free
Bed and Breakfast	Twin/double	£55	1 free
	Family	£75	2 free

Figure 38 Compare this with Figure 37: the column widths have been adjusted

Inserting and deleting columns and rows

In Figure 39 an extra column has been added to the table to show the midweek prices. Extra rows have also been added to enable the headings to become part of the table and to separate the two different categories of accommodation. Extra columns and rows can be inserted by selecting **Table, Insert**.

HOTEL STOPOVERS				
ALL OFFERS SUBJECT TO AVAILABILITY				
Category	**Accommodation**	**Weekend**	**Midweek**	**Extra Child**
Room only	Twin/double	£35	£35	N/A
	Family	£45	£45	2 free
Bed and Breakfast	Twin/double	£55	£60	1 free
	Family	£75	£80	2 free
Prices shown in £s per room				

Figure 39 Compare this with Figure 38: the table now has an extra column, and four additional rows have been inserted

Text boxes

A *text box* is a drawing object that contains text. You can format the text in a text box in the same way as any other text in your document, but because it is contained in a box you can resize it and move it. You can use a text box to realign text and can add shadow and 3-D styles.

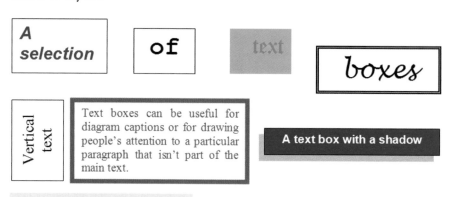

Figure 40 A selection of text boxes

You can add a text box by selecting **Insert, Text Box** from the menu, or by using the **Text Box** icon on the *Drawing* toolbar. You must then click and drag your mouse over the area in which you want the text box to appear.

Creating, selecting and inserting components

Types of components

Many of the publications you produce may comprise more than one component, such as

- images
- lines and simple shapes
- tick boxes
- comments
- hyperlinks.

You must remember that whatever you include in a publication should be there because it improves the effectiveness of that publication and not just because you felt like putting something in.

Images

Images used to illustrate a topic can certainly help people to understand the topic and generally make a publication more interesting for the reader. However, you should only include images that are fully relevant to the topic and that serve a purpose by being included.

You may search through a picture library to find a relevant image, but you must be very careful to obtain permission to use the image if it is protected by copyright laws. Images taken with a digital camera can be inserted directly from the camera. Photographs and images in books and magazines or photographs you take with a traditional camera will need to be scanned into the document.

Remember to record full details of the sources of all images you include in your work.

Lines and simple shapes

You will find it very useful to investigate the *Drawing* toolbar and to experiment with the variety of lines and shapes that are available for you to use. Move your mouse pointer over the toolbar to see the names given to the various tools.

Figure 41 The Drawing toolbar

✔ **TiP**

If you find it difficult to place one object in front of another, use the Order option in the Draw menu to send an object in front or behind another.

✔ **TiP**

If you hold down the Ctrl key whilst using the arrow directional keys, you can 'nudge' the lines and shapes across the screen in very small steps. If you increase the zoom on the screen to 200% or 500% you can see very clearly when lines and shapes are in the right position.

Skills check ▷▷

See the Artwork and Imaging skills chapter for more details about grouping and ungrouping (page 143)

The arrow tool is very helpful if you need to label a diagram. Other shapes can be built up to form a variety of objects.

The image of the train in Figure 42 is made up from approximately 30 lines and shapes. Some have been copied, some have been filled with colour and all lines have been made thicker.

Figure 42 A train constructed from simple shapes

Grouping and ungrouping

You have produced an image that is made up of many different lines and shapes. If you try to move the image, it will be impossible to keep all the shapes together unless you *group* them. Grouping allows you to treat a group of objects as a single object that can be rotated, resized or flipped. Any group of images can be *ungrouped* and treated as a number of separate objects again.

Borders

You may sometimes wish to place a border round a full page, for example on a poster. You will find a wide choice of artwork and line styles available in **Format, Borders and Shading, Page Border**.

You can use the *Rectangle* tool to place a border around an image or object. Draw the rectangle shape over the image with the **Rectangle** tool on the *Drawing* toolbar. The image will disappear under the rectangle but you can double-click the rectangle, remove the 'Fill' colour and choose a suitable line style and colour. You can resize the rectangle as necessary.

Tick boxes

Tick boxes are useful on questionnaires and surveys if you are supplying a set of choices and you want people to tick one or more boxes. You will find a selection of tick (or check) boxes through **Insert, Symbol, Wingdings**. To increase their size, treat them like any other character symbol.

Figure 43 Characters useful for tick boxes

Comments

You know it is essential that your work is reviewed regularly by a wide range of people and that you should consider carefully any comments your reviewers make. Sometimes it may be convenient to ask your reviewer to look at a printed version of your work. In that case your reviewer might write his or her comments down or talk them over with you.

However, there may be occasions when you send a copy of your work by email if the reviewer is not nearby, for example if he or she is a member of a specialist group or team. The reviewer can use the 'comments' feature of your word processor to insert his or her thoughts directly into the document file. The file can then be emailed back to you and the comments will be on-screen for you to consider. This can save a lot of time for a reviewer.

You will also find comments useful for you to use as your projects develop. If you have a change of mind about something, you can insert a comment into the document explaining and justifying your reasons. This can then be presented as evidence in your e-portfolio.

Hyperlinks

You have learnt how to insert and use hyperlinks in web pages. You can insert hyperlinks in word-processed documents too. For example in your e-portfolio you might have a series of versions of a document showing all of its development stages; you can use hyperlinks to take you from one version of the document to another. Imagine how effective it will be for your assessors to follow the progress and read your comments as each element of your project is considered.

Styles

When you open your word processor, you know that some things will always be the same. For example

- the first letter is always positioned in the same place on the page
- the font size and style is always the same
- the line spacing is always single
- paragraph alignment is always left aligned or left justified.

This style of presentation is the default or *Normal* style, which always presents itself when you open a new document.

The current style is displayed through the *Style* button ![Normal] and if you click on this you will be able to see the styles available.

A style can be any combination of formatting characteristics that you name and store as a set, such as font style, font size, margin settings and page orientation. When you apply a style, all the formatting instructions in that style are applied at one time. Any style can be created and saved to suit the requirements of a particular document. For example, if certain documents must always be set up in Comic Sans 14 pt, double line spacing with centre justification then it would be sensible to set a style so that you don't have to reformat the standard features every time you need to create such a document. You would just select the style from the stored list.

You could set a style to add a defined space after headings and paragraphs. Choose, **Format, Paragraph** and insert the required point-sized space against 'After'. For example, a 6 pt space after all headings is the equivalent to $\frac{1}{2}$ clear line space if you are working in a 12 pt font size.

Use styles to improve the overall appearance of your documents, to help retain consistency of presentation throughout and to make them smarter.

Using images and objects

Many documents and on-screen presentations contain illustrations. These are included to help simplify the information in the text, or to provide decoration. In this book many types of illustrations have been used: pictures, photographs, charts, screen prints, text boxes, clip art, WordArt, etc. Collectively these are referred to as *objects*.

Sensible use of images will greatly improve a document (see Figure 44). An image or object can be inserted by selecting the **Insert** drop-down menu.

TRAVELBUG WATER SPORTS

Departing 20 June
Travel by luxury coach from Whychton
14 nights half-board accommodation in 3-star hotel

A fantastic opportunity to experience a variety of water sports including:

Windsurfing

Learn the basics of windsurfing, including rigging, equipment care, sailing across the wind and self-rescue. Advanced skills include instruction on topics such as water starts, harness use, and shortboards. Wetsuits and windsurfing gear are provided.

Snorkelling

For many people the water's edge is the limit of their activity and knowledge. Learn to snorkel and enjoy the world that lurks beneath the surface of the water. You will be introduced to snorkelling equipment including the mask, flippers and snorkel and will learn how to move safely in the water.

Water skiing

If you are a complete beginner you will start on land and learn the fundamentals of body position, technique and safety. Once you and your instructor are confident in understanding the basics on land, you move to the water. First-time skiers will use the static boom on the side of the boat to offer stability. When you have mastered the boom, then it is off to the long line! Who knows, you may be able to Slalom, Trick or Jump before the end of your holiday!

£585 per person

(based on two people sharing a room and fully inclusive of all equipment and tuition)

17 London Road   Whychton   TO9 3WN

Tel: 543 2134 5678   www.travelbug.co.uk
Fax: 543 2134 5679   Email: info@travelbug.co.uk

Figure 44 Sensible use of images will greatly improve a document and make it more appealing to the target audience

Positioning images and objects

Any image in a document should be there to serve a specific purpose, and its positioning is therefore very important. The position of the cursor when the image is inserted into the document will determine where it appears. Figure 45 shows an example. After the image was inserted, the text was pushed down the page.

Windsurfing

Learn the basics of windsurfing, including rigging, equipment care, sailing across the wind and self-rescue. Advanced skills include instruction on topics such as water starts, harness use, and shortboards. Wetsuits and windsurfing gear are provided.

Windsurfing

Learn the basics of windsurfing, including rigging, equipment care, sailing across the wind and self-rescue. Advanced skills include instruction on topics such as water starts, harness use, and shortboards. Wetsuits and windsurfing gear are provided.

Figure 45 An example of text before the insertion of an image, and the same text with an image: notice how the text has been pushed down the page

Wrapping text around an image

As you can see from Figure 45, although an image has been placed in the document, its inclusion does not really improve the document because it is positioned on the left with empty space at the side. In order to make the document more interesting and the image more manageable, you can format the image and select a *wrapping style* to improve the layout. Figure 46 shows two examples.

Figure 46 A 'square' wrapping style, and a 'tight' wrapping style in which the text hugs the edges of the image

 TiP

You should make sure that any images you include in your documents improve their appearance and are not included just because you fancied putting them in!

Wrapping of an image can be achieved by selecting the **Format, Picture** (or **Object**), **Layout** drop-down menu.

Images and objects that are formatted to wrap text can also be moved more easily within the document by clicking and dragging them to a new position.

Sizing an image

Sometimes the size of an image or object should be restricted because of the amount of available space on the page. Any object can be resized by selecting the object to show the selection handles and dragging one of the handles with the mouse.

TiP

Take care when resizing an image. If you select a corner handle the image will be resized while retaining its true proportions. However, if you select a centre top, bottom or side handle you could end up with images looking like Figure 47.

Figure 47 Images that have been resized without retaining the original proportions: inclusion of these images would not improve a document!

(a)

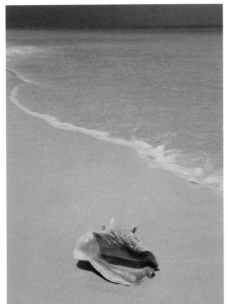

Cropping an image

From time to time an image we require might be part of a larger image. We can 'crop' the unwanted area from the image by using the **Crop** tool in the *Picture* toolbar.

(c)

(b)

Figure 48 (a) A clip art image of a sea shell on the beach. (b) The sea shell has been 'cropped', removing the surrounding area. (c) The cropped image can then be resized if necessary.

Using spelling and grammar checkers

The importance of using spelling and grammar checkers has been stressed in Standard Ways of Working (on page 73).

As a student on an IT course, you have no excuse for submitting work which contains spelling and grammar errors – the tools to help you check the accuracy of your work are at your fingertips. Make sure nothing is left unchecked!

Using mail merge

Jargon buster

Mail merge is used when an organisation wishes to send the same letter to a large number of people.

Many of the letters that arrive in the post at your home will have been prepared using a process called *mail merge*. The letters will appear to have been addressed personally to their recipients, but in fact each letter will probably have been produced as part of a large batch of many letters, all containing exactly the same message but addressed to different people.

This is a very quick and easy way of contacting customers, whose details may be held on a company database. These letters are often sent from banks, building societies, insurance companies, large retail stores, utility companies, credit card companies and other financial businesses.

⍰ Think it over ...

Think of five occasions your family might have received letters produced using mail merge.

How are the letters produced?

The letters are produced in two stages – refer to pages 132–136 of the D201 DiDA book if you don't remember the exact process.

- First, a *data file* which contains the personal information of the recipients is required. This may be an existing database, or it might be produced in a word-processing or spreadsheet file for a one-off mail merge operation. It will contain details such as name, address, telephone number and account number.

- Second, a *standard letter* is produced. This will contain the text of the message. Instead of being addressed in the usual way, it will contain what are called *merge fields*.

Jargon buster

Merge fields are the points at which the individual personalised details will be inserted in each letter.

Spreadsheet software

You will almost certainly have used a spreadsheet for your schoolwork. You will know that the main purpose of a spreadsheet is to enter, edit and manipulate *numerical* data, and to *make calculations* using this data. As part of your e-portfolio evidence for your coursework, you will need to gather and analyse data to produce meaningful information, some of which will be in the form of spreadsheets and graphs or charts.

Spreadsheet programs make it much easier to perform financial tasks such as calculating staff wages, profit made on goods sold, VAT (value-added tax) returns for the government, and bank accounts. A spreadsheet program is an invaluable tool to all kinds of organisations, from small ones such as a neighbourhood card shop, to your own school or college, or huge companies such as Top Shop, Microsoft or government organisations such as the National Health Service.

On a personal level you might use a spreadsheet to keep track of how much income you receive, what expenses you have and how much is left to save.

LEARNING OUTCOMES

You need to learn about
- ✓ entering, cutting, copying, pasting and moving data
- ✓ formatting cells to match data types
- ✓ using operators
- ✓ replicating formulas using relative cell references
- ✓ replicating formulas using absolute cell references
- ✓ inserting or deleting rows and columns
- ✓ using simple functions
- ✓ sorting data
- ✓ producing fully customised charts and graphs
- ✓ using headers and footers
- ✓ printing selected areas
- ✓ **inserting comments**
- ✓ **filtering data**
- ✓ **linking sheets.**

Entering, cutting, copying, pasting and moving data

Let's look at the structure of spreadsheets in more detail, beginning with a very basic example.

The spreadsheet worksheet is divided into *rows* and *columns*, creating a *grid of cells*. Each row and column in a spreadsheet is given a unique number or letter, so each cell can be identified rather like a map reference – A1, B6, C12 etc.

	A	B	C	D
1				
2				
3				
4				

Figure 49 Spreadsheet cell references

Cell C2

The data – a row or column heading, text or number – is entered into a cell. However, the default size of a cell is quite small. If the data entered into the cell is too wide it will overlap into the next cell; but as soon as data is entered into the adjacent cell, some of the original data becomes hidden (not lost). You will then need to decide the best method of overcoming the problem, and this is discussed later.

After you start using a spreadsheet you may need to make changes because

- you have identified some improvements you could introduce
- you have learned more about the spreadsheet program's facilities
- the needs of the business have altered.

You can cut, copy, paste and move data between cells, rows and columns. Look back at page 85 – you will see that the icons and keystrokes work in exactly the same way in Excel.

Formatting cells to match their data types

Unless formatting techniques (use of bold, colour, borders, fill or shading) have been used, the spreadsheet can be very difficult to read – especially if it is very large, covering many rows and columns. So it is very important to consider the *appearance* of the spreadsheet as well as the data and the formulas.

Just as in word-processing software, you can enhance the text in a spreadsheet by

- using bold, italic or underlined text
- varying the font size for main headings or sub-headings
- using different font styles.

In addition you can improve the appearance of the spreadsheet by

- formatting a heading at an angle or vertically within cells
- centring a heading horizontally within a cell or across two or more columns
- centring a heading vertically within a cell (i.e. centred from top to bottom)
- wrapping text within a cell to avoid having an extremely wide column
- adjusting the cell width or height
- highlighting significant cells (e.g. ones with totals) with borders or colours.

Figure 50 Angled headings

You should also pay attention to the following when formatting numerical data:

- How many decimal places do you need, if any? For example, if you have a column for the number of students in different tutor groups, you would not have $\frac{1}{2}$ or 0.5 of a student! However, if you are listing the sales of fruit or vegetables, you might well have $\frac{1}{2}$ or 0.5 of a kilo. In the first case you do not need any decimal places, but in the second you might well want to show two decimal places.
- If the data is the cost of the item, do you wish to show the currency symbol, or is it enough to format the money to two decimal places? What would be suitable for house prices?
- If the currency symbol is used, is it too cluttered to show the £ sign everywhere, or might it be better to use it just for the totals?
- Do you wish to show negative numbers in red? If so, this can be set automatically.

Columns marked A, B, C etc.

Rows marked 1,2, 3 etc.

Notice text that is partially hidden by data in the next cell

Column headings

Data entered into the cells

Figure 51 Whychton Stationers invoice to Travelbug: a very basic spreadsheet layout before quantity, unit price and formulas have been entered

Entering and using formulas

If you go into a sweetshop and buy three bars of chocolate at 50p each, you know that the total cost will be £1.50, but how would you work that out? You multiplied 3 by 50, and that was your *formula.*

Using operators

The important point to remember is that in Excel *a formula always starts with an equals sign.* This tells Excel that it needs to perform a calculation. In order to tell the spreadsheet what kind of calculation you need, you use the following *arithemetic operators*:

- adding +
- multiplying *
- subtracting –
- dividing /

The spreadsheet will calculate formulas using *values*, such as

	Formula	Result
Formula using values	=40*5.99	239.60

More typically, *cell references* are used in formulas. For example, in cell E15 in Figure 51 you would use the formula '=C15*D15' to calculate the cost of the A4 copy paper

	Formula	Result
Formula using cell references	=C15*D15	239.60

The big advantage with using cell references in formulas, rather than the actual numbers, is that the spreadsheet will automatically do a recalculation if any changes are made in the data. For example, if the price of the paper changes to £6.50, you enter the new price in cell D15 and the total cost will be automatically recalculated (£260).

Figure 52 shows the Travelbug invoice from Figure 51 with the formulas inserted in column E.

	A	B	C	D	E
1	Whychton Sta				
2	45 London Rd				
3	Whychton				
4	TO9 9WN				
5	Tel: 543 7895				
6	Fax: 543 789				
7	E-mail: Whyc				
8	Customer				
9	Name	Travelbug		Invoice No:	WS1001
10	Address	17 London Road		Account No	0001
11	Town	Whychton		Order No:	TB465
12	Post Code	TO9 3WN		Date:	19/01/20-
13					
14	Product Ref	Description	Quantity	Unit Price	Total
15	1289	A4 copy paper	40	5.99	=C15*D15
16	4573	Sticky message pa	12	3.99	=C16*D16
17	1823	Post-it pads	24	2.99	=C17*D17
18	9871	Diary - 1 day to a p	2	12.99	=C18*D18
19	4622	Stapler - heavy duty	1	24.99	=C19*D19
20				Sub Total	=SUM(E15:E19)
21				lers £300 +	=E20*3%
22				Sub Total	=E20-E21
23				Vat	=E22*17.5%
24				Total	=E22+E23

Figure 52 Travelbug invoice showing the formulas

Replicating formulas

Using relative cell references

The spreadsheet designed for Whychton Stationers had only a few formulas, so it did not take long to enter them into the cells.

However, as already mentioned, spreadsheets used by business organisations can be huge, and it would be very tedious to enter the same formula across 100 rows or down 100 columns:

=SUM(C5:E5)
=SUM(C6:E6)
...
...
=SUM(C105:E105)!

One of the advantages of using a spreadsheet is the facility to *replicate* (i.e. copy) a formula across columns or down rows, rather than having to keep entering it again and again. If you need to have totals down several rows or across several columns, you can enter the formula into the first cell and then replicate the formula across to the last column or down to the last row. The spreadsheet will automatically change the formula to give the correct cell references.

Look back at Figure 52, where you can see the formula in cell E15 to calculate the total is '=C15*D15'. You could then enter the formula on the next row by keying in '=C16*D16', and so on down each row. However, once the formula is entered into cell E15, as it is copied down the rows the software automatically changes the cell references to '=C16*D16', '=C17*D17' and so on.

Using absolute cell references

Sometimes you wish to refer to a particular cell address many times. Therefore when you replicate the formula, the *cell address needs to remain the same*. The technical term for this is *absolute reference*.

Figure 53 illustrates this point. Travelbug have a number of villas for holiday rentals in different parts of Europe. As more and more customers are making enquiries via the Internet, Travelbug realised that it was important to quote prices in both pounds and euros. The price in euros is calculated by multiplying the price in pounds by the rate of exchange. The rate of exchange is entered in one cell: D2. In this case, as the formula is copied down the rows, the cell reference for the price in sterling needs to change from row to row, *but the cell reference for the rate of exchange – D2 – needs to remain the same*.

You will notice that the formulas in column E show $ signs before the D and 2 (note D2 in Figure 53). These signs are used in Excel to instruct the program that, when copying the formula, this cell reference must *not* be changed. Although in the small example

	A	B	C	D	E
1			**Travelbug Villas**		
2			of Exchange £ to €	1.4	
3	**Destination**	**Resort**	**Name of Villa**	**Price per week Sterling**	**Price per week Euros**
4	Algarve	Bordeira	Casa Luz	799	=D4*D2
5	Algarve	Lagos	Casa Limoa	849	=D5*D2
6	Algarve	Estol	Casa Marco	719	=D6*D2
7	Algarve	Carvoeiro	Sete Estrelo	899	=D7*D2
8	Cyprus	Latchi	Irene	859	=D8*D2
9	Cyprus	Coral Bay	Villa Olivia	809	=D9*D2
10	Cyprus	Polis	The Vines	909	=D10*D2
11	Costa Blanca	Denia	Casa Moura	779	=D11*D2
12	Costa Blanca	Javea	Las Palmmares	829	=D12*D2
13	Costa Blanca	Calpe	Casa Alana	779	=D13*D2
14	Costa Blanca	Albir	Villa Marlene	649	=D14*D2
15	France	Dordogne	Eva	2225	=D15*D2
16	France	Dordogne	Chateau Alexa	1490	=D16*D2
17	France	Cote D'Azur	La Marina	2720	=D17*D2
18	France	South West Coast	Villa Zivia	1660	=D18*D2
19	France	West Coast - Charentes	La Belle Vacance	965	=D19*D2

Figure 53 The formula view of the price list for renting Travelbug villas: notice that the cell reference D4 changes to D5, etc., but the cell reference D2 does not

shown it would be easy to key in the formula on each new line, as mentioned already, in a commercial spreadsheet you might replicate the formula down hundreds of rows. The other benefit is that, when the rate of exchange alters, it is a simple matter to enter the new rate in cell D2 and all prices in column E will change automatically.

Figure 54 shows the spreadsheet after the calculations have been done by the software.

	A	B	C	D	E
1			**Travelbug Villas**		
2			**Rate of Exchange £ to €**	**€ 1.40**	
3	**Destination**	**Resort**	**Name of Villa**	**Price per week Sterling**	**Price per week Euros**
4	Algarve	Bordeira	Casa Luz	£799	€ 1,119
5	Algarve	Lagos	Casa Limoa	£849	€ 1,189
6	Algarve	Estol	Casa Marco	£719	€ 1,007
7	Algarve	Carvoeiro	Sete Estrelo	£899	€ 1,259
8	Cyprus	Latchi	Irene	£859	€ 1,203
9	Cyprus	Coral Bay	Villa Olivia	£809	€ 1,133
10	Cyprus	Polis	The Vines	£909	€ 1,273
11	Costa Blanca	Denia	Casa Moura	£779	€ 1,091
12	Costa Blanca	Javea	Las Palmmares	£829	€ 1,161
13	Costa Blanca	Calpe	Casa Alana	£779	€ 1,091
14	Costa Blanca	Albir	Villa Marlene	£649	€ 909
15	France	Dordogne	Eva	£2,225	€ 3,115
16	France	Dordogne	Chateau Alexa	£1,490	€ 2,086
17	France	Cote D'Azur	La Marina	£2,720	€ 3,808
18	France	South West Coast	Villa Zivia	£1,660	€ 2,324
19	France	West Coast - Charentes	La Belle Vacance	£965	€ 1,351

Figure 54 The data view of the price list for renting Travelbug villas

Inserting or deleting rows and columns

Spreadsheet software makes it easy to add or delete rows or columns. To delete cells, select them and then use the **Delete** command on the right-click menu. To insert cells, select the location where you want to add them and use the options on the **Insert** menu.

Using simple functions

When you open an Excel worksheet and click on the function icon , you will see that there are very many functions available. We shall look here at two frequently used functions – SUM and AVERAGE.

The SUM function

Look back at Figure 52 on page 111 and the formula in cell E20. Remember that the formula could have been written as '=E15+E16+E17+E18+E19'. That becomes very tedious if you have to add up 100 rows or columns, and it is easy to make mistakes, but by using the SUM function you can add up the range of cells without having to enter each cell reference.

You can use the SUM function by keying in a formula – in this case '=SUM(E15:E19)'. The colon (:) tells the program to add up all the cells in the range from E15 to E19.

It can be quicker to use the **Autosum** icon Σ on the *Standard* toolbar.

Usually the correct range of cells will be selected, but do be careful when using **AutoSum**: sometimes cells are included that are not required.

Look at Figure 55, where the **AutoSum** command was used in cell F5 to calculate the total number of weeks reserved. The range selected was 'B5:E5', but *this includes the cost of weekly rental* as well as the weeks reserved in each of the three months. To calculate the total number of weeks, only the range 'C5:E5' is necessary. To correct the error you can either enter '=SUM(C5:E5)' yourself, or select cells C5 to E5 by dragging with the mouse. You can then copy the formulas down the rows using relative cell references, as you learned earlier.

AutoSum command

Figure 55 The AutoSum command and four worksheets in the workbook: the status line near the top shows the incorrect formula '=SUM(B5:E5)' selected by the AutoSum command

Quite often, students enter '=SUM' as part of a formula when it is not necessary. Look back at Figure 52 (page 111). The formula in cell E24 is '=E22+E23', but students sometimes enter '=SUM(E22:E23)'. This will work, but it is *not* required in this case.

The AVERAGE function

When you calculate the average, you are trying to establish the typical value of a group or situation. You do this by adding up all the relevant items and dividing by the number of items. For example, if you wanted to find out the average rental price of the villas, you would add up all the prices and divide by the number of villas in the list.

Look at Figure 56. The formula '=AVERAGE(F5:F20)' is entered into cell F21, and this calculates the average cost to rent a villa for a week. You will notice that none of the villas costs £727 to rent, but this was the *average* or typical cost in the low season.

If you were working out the average cost of rental yourself, you would need to add up the cost to rent all the villas (£11 629), and divide by the number of villas in the list (16) to find the average (£727). The advantage of using the AVERAGE function is that these various stages are all worked out automatically for you.

	A	B	C	D	E	F	G	H	I
1			Travelbug Villas						
2		Rate of Exchange £ to €		€ 1.40					
3						Low Season		High Season	
4	Destination	Resort	Name of Villa	No of bedrooms	Sleeps up to	Price per week Sterling	Price per week Euros	Price per week Sterling	Price per week Euros
5	Algarve	Bordeira	Casa Luz	3	6	£559	€ 783	£799	€ 1,119
6	Algarve	Lagos	Casa Limoa	3	6	£594	€ 832	£849	€ 1,189
7	Algarve	Estol	Casa Marco	2	4	£503	€ 704	£719	€ 1,007
8	Algarve	Carvoeiro	Sete Estrelo	4	8	£629	€ 881	£899	€ 1,259
9	Cyprus	Latchi	Irene	4	8	£601	€ 841	£859	€ 1,203
10	Cyprus	Coral Bay	Villa Olivia	3	6	£566	€ 792	£809	€ 1,133
11	Cyprus	Polis	The Vines	5	10	£636	€ 890	£909	€ 1,273
12	Cyprus	Argaka	Agathi	4	8	£629	€ 881	£859	€ 1,203
13	Costa Blanca	Denia	Casa Moura	4	8	£545	€ 763	£779	€ 1,091
14	Costa Blanca	Javea	Las Palmmares	4	8	£580	€ 812	£829	€ 1,161
15	Costa Blanca	Calpe	Casa Alana	3	6	£545	€ 763	£779	€ 1,091
16	Costa Blanca	Albir	Villa Marlene	2	4	£454	€ 636	£649	€ 909
17	France	Dordogne	Chateau Alexa	4	8	£1,043	€ 1,460	£1,490	€ 2,086
18	France	Cote D'Azur	La Marina	5	10	£1,904	€ 2,666	£2,720	€ 3,808
19	France	South West Coast	Villa Zivia	4	8	£1,162	€ 1,627	£1,660	€ 2,324
20	France	West Coast - Charentes	La Belle Vacance	2	4	£675	€ 945	£965	€ 1,351
21			Average price of weekly rental			£727	€ 1,017	£1,036	€ 1,450

Figure 56 Spreadsheet showing calculated average weekly rentals

Sorting data

It can often be useful to sort the data in the spreadsheet *alphabetically* (from A to Z or from Z to A), or *numerically* (from lowest to highest or from highest to lowest). You can use **Data**, **Sort** from Excel's menu to sort your data.

Inserting comments

Sometimes it can be helpful to add comments to the spreadsheet. These comments do not print, but are an on-screen guide to help the user. This would be a useful method to remind Whychton Stationers' administrator to call the customer if the order is less than £300 (Whychton Stationers offer a discount on orders over £300).

In order to add a comment in Excel, place the cursor in the cell where you wish the comment to appear and select **Insert**, **Comment** (Figure 57). A box will appear in which you can write a suitable message (Figure 58).

A small red triangle in the corner of the cell shows that the cell contains a comment. The default setting usually shows the indicator only, but the message appears when the mouse pointer is over the

Figure 57 Using the Insert sub-menu to insert a comment

cell. However, you can choose to show the indicator (the small red triangle) and the message by selecting **Tools, Options** and then the **View** tab (Figure 59).

Figure 58 The box in which to write your comment

Figure 59 To show the comment as well as the indicator, click in the circle

Go out and try!

1 Open the file saved as 'Travelbug invoice' and click in cell E22 containing the sub-total.
2 Add the comment box 'Call customer if sub-total is less than £300'.
3 Change the setting to show the indicator and the message.
4 💾 Save the file.

Open your 'Spreadsheet software' file. Create a new bold heading called '**SS Activity 4.1**' and write a short paragraph describing the skills you have demonstrated in this activity, under the heading 'Comment boxes'. 💾 Save the file.

Filtering data

The *filter tool* 🔽▪ is a method of displaying more precisely the information you require just at that moment. For example, you might wish to find items in a certain category or to a specific value, or the top ten items in a list. By using the filter to select the relevant criteria, the spreadsheet will filter out everything that does not match the criteria.

Imagine that your phone bill arrives and is much higher than usual. You want to find out exactly how much you have spent on calling landlines, on foreign calls and on mobile numbers. You could scan the bill into the spreadsheet and then use the filter tool to separate the various charges.

Figure 60 shows a small section of a telephone bill that runs to 219 rows in total. The total bill for the month is £38.37. By clicking on the arrow next to the destination, it is possible to select 'Usa' (United States), with the result that only calls to the United States will be shown. Figure 61 illustrates the result – the total cost was £5.43.

Look at the row numbers. See how they jump from 1 to 5 to 13 etc., because all rows not containing the text Usa are now hidden.

Click here to select the type of filter to apply.

D	E	F
DESTINATION ▼	**TIME** ▼	**COST** ▼
UK Mobile	00:43:21	£1.97
Freephone	00:00:06	£0.00
UK Mobile	00:25:03	£2.96
Usa	00:01:37	£0.05
Local	00:09:15	£0.00
UK Mobile	00:02:18	£0.34
Freephone	00:08:56	£0.00
UK Mobile	00:01:03	£0.29
UK Mobile	00:10:19	£1.25
UK Mobile	00:00:27	£0.14
Local	00:01:04	£0.04
Usa	00:28:31	£0.74
Local	00:06:33	£0.15
Local	00:00:53	£0.02
UK Mobile	00:00:04	£0.15
UK Mobile	00:05:19	£0.68
Usa	00:25:47	£0.66
Local	00:09:55	£0.00
Local	00:06:51	£0.00
Local	00:00:34	£0.00
National	00:29:09	£0.64
Local	00:18:19	£0.00
Usa	00:22:54	£0.59
Local	00:00:04	£0.00
Local	00:00:49	£0.00
UK Mobile	00:00:21	£0.11
Local	00:01:20	£0.00

Figure 60 A small part of an itemised phone bill

	D	E	F
1	**DESTINATION** ▼	**TIME** ▼	**COST** ▼
5	(All)	00:01:37	£0.05
13	(Top 10...)	00:28:31	£0.74
18	(Custom...)	00:25:47	£0.66
24	Australia	00:22:54	£0.59
29	Freephone	00:00:41	£0.03
30	Local	00:16:47	£0.43
	National		
54	UK Mobile	00:00:34	£0.03
62	Usa	00:13:11	£0.36
96	Usa	00:00:58	£0.03
114	Usa	00:13:09	£0.36
115	Usa	00:00:03	£0.03
116	Usa	00:00:52	£0.03
127	Usa	00:05:15	£0.15
128	Usa	00:00:59	£0.03
129	Usa	00:00:09	£0.03
131	Usa	00:00:27	£0.03
146	Usa	00:17:02	£0.41
147	Usa	00:17:02	£0.05
149	Usa	00:00:39	£0.03
150	Usa	00:00:45	£0.03
151	Usa	00:02:19	£0.08
153	Usa	00:17:10	£0.46
167	Usa	00:20:31	£0.54
172	Usa	00:04:45	£0.13
184	Usa	00:02:58	£0.08
203	Usa	00:00:40	£0.03
204	Usa	00:00:33	£0.03
205	Usa	00:00:28	£0.03
206	Usa	00:00:34	£0.03
234	**Total**	**215 Mins**	**5.43**

Figure 61 The list of calls has been filtered to show only those made to the United States

Go out and try!

1 Open the spreadsheet file saved as 'Villa rentals'. You want to identify which villas are having very few rentals in the first quarter. Whilst this is easy to see with such a small spreadsheet, it would be much more difficult if the company were letting a large number of villas.

2 Select the worksheet for the 1st Quarter and highlight the column headings in row 4 – cells A4 to G4. Click on the filter icon ▽₌; if it is not available then select **Data**, **Filter**, **AutoFilter** from the menu. Notice that arrows appear next to each of the column headings, as shown in Figure 62.

	A	B	C	D	E	F	G
1			**Travelbug Villas**				
2	**Quarterly Rentals**						
3	**Low Season**		**Number of weeks reserved**				
4	**Name of Villa** ▾	**Cost of weekly rental** ▾	**Jan** ▾	**Feb** ▾	**Mar** ▾	**Total No Weeks Reserved** ▾	**Total Value of Booking** ▾
5	Villa Olivia	£566	4	4	3	(All)	£6,229
6	Irene	£601	3	2	4	(Top 10...)	£5,412
7	The Vines	£636	2	2	3	(Custom...)	£4,454
8	Villa Marlene	£454	3	1	3	1 3 5	£3,180
9	Casa Limoa	£594	1	2	3	6	£3,566
10	Casa Marco	£503	1	1	4	7 9	£3,020
11	Sete Estrelo	£629	3	1	2	11	£3,776
12	Las Palmmares	£580	2	1	3	89	£3,482

Figure 62 First-quarter worksheet showing the filter options for the number of weeks reserved

3 To identify those villas with only one week reserved, click on the down arrow in column F and then select **1**. All other villas will be filtered out.

4 Select the worksheet for the 2nd Quarter and this time click on the down arrow in column G and then select **(Top 10...)** (Figure 63) and **OK**. The top ten values will be filtered.

Figure 63 The Top Ten AutoFilter

5 Select the worksheet for the 3rd Quarter and identify those villas that were not booked for the full 12 weeks. To do this, click on the down arrow in column F and then select **(Custom...)**. Select **is less than** and **12** and click **OK** (Figure 64). All villas booked for 12 weeks will be filtered out.

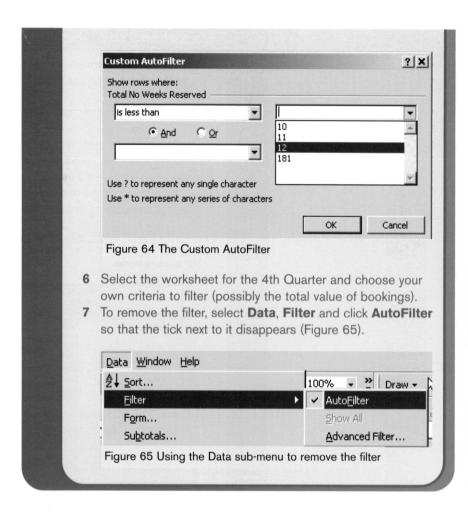

Figure 64 The Custom AutoFilter

6 Select the worksheet for the 4th Quarter and choose your own criteria to filter (possibly the total value of bookings).

7 To remove the filter, select **Data**, **Filter** and click **AutoFilter** so that the tick next to it disappears (Figure 65).

Figure 65 Using the Data sub-menu to remove the filter

Open your 'Spreadsheet software' file. Create a new bold heading called '**SS Activity 4.2 – Filtering data**' and write a short paragraph describing the skills you have demonstrated in this activity. Save the file.

Linking worksheets

It can often be useful to *link worksheets* so that a value on one worksheet is carried forward to another. The advantages of linking the data, rather than copying it into a new sheet, are that there is no risk of making a copying error and if the original data changes then the cells in the linked sheets will be automatically updated.

Go out and try!

TiP

To create a new worksheet, right-click any of the worksheet tabs and select **Insert** from the menu that appears. With **Worksheet** selected, press **OK**. Double-click the new tab to rename it.

1 Open the spreadsheet file 'Villa rentals' and select each quarter's worksheet in turn. *Make sure that the filters are removed from all the worksheets.* Sort each worksheet into alphabetical order of the name of the villa.
   ○ Highlight cells A4 to G20.
   ○ Click on the A–Z sort icon on the *Standard* toolbar.
   ○ Repeat these two steps for each of the quarterly worksheets and then save the file.

2 Start a new worksheet named 'Summary' and enter the headings shown in Figure 66. Now you are going to create links between the Summary worksheet and the quarterly worksheets.

	A	B	C	D	E	F	G	H	I	J	K
1				Travelbug Villas							
2		1st Quarter		2nd Quarter		3rd Quarter		4th Quarter		Year	
3	Name of Villa	Total No Weeks Reserved	Total Value of Bookings	Total No Weeks Reserved	Total Value of Bookings	Total No Weeks Reserved	Total Value of Bookings	Total No Weeks Reserved	Total Value of Bookings	Total No Weeks Reserved	Total Value of Bookings

Figure 66 Headings for the Summary worksheet

A4		= ='1st Quarter'!A5
	A	B	C

	A	B	C
1			Travelk
2		1st Quarter	
3	Name of Villa	Total No Weeks Reserved	Total Value of Bookings
4	Agathi	5	£3,145

Figure 67 Formula for the link between worksheets

3 On the Summary worksheet, click on cell A4 and type an equals sign (=). Do **not** press **Enter** yet.

4 Click on the 1st Quarter worksheet tab, then on cell A5, and press **Enter**. The formula will be **='1st Quarter'!A5**, but the name of the villa (Agathi) will appear in the cell (Figure 67). Copy the formula down the rows until the name of the last villa appears – Villa Zivia.

5 Repeat this process for the total number of weeks reserved and the total value of bookings for each of the four quarters. Figure 68 will start you off.

	A	B	C	D
1				Travelbug Villa
2		1st Quarter		2nd Q
3	Name of Villa	Total No Weeks Reserved	Total Value of Bookings	Total No Weeks Reserved
4	='1st Quarter'!A5	='1st Quarter'!F5	='1st Quarter'!G5	=2nd Quarter'!F5
5	='1st Quarter'!A6	='1st Quarter'!F6	='1st Quarter'!G6	=2nd Quarter'!F6
6	='1st Quarter'!A7	='1st Quarter'!F7	='1st Quarter'!G7	=2nd Quarter'!F7

Figure 68 Section of the spreadsheet showing the formulas for columns A to D

6 Enter formulas to calculate the total number of weeks reserved and the total value of bookings for the year for each villa. Then calculate the grand totals.

7 The Summary spreadsheet should now look like the one shown in Figure 69.

	A	B	C	D	E	F	G	H	I	J	K
1		Travelbug Villas									
2		1st Quarter		2nd Quarter		3rd Quarter		4th Quarter		Year	
3	Name of Villa	Total No Weeks Reserved	Total Value of Bookings	Total No Weeks Reserved	Total Value of Bookings	Total No Weeks Reserved	Total Value of Bookings	Total No Weeks Reserved	Total Value of Bookings	Total No Weeks Reserved	Total Value of Bookings
4	Agathi	5	£3,145	11	£9,449	12	£10,308	5	£3,145	33	£26,047
5	Casa Alana	5	£2,725	7	£5,453	11	£8,569	10	£5,450	33	£22,197
6	Casa Limoa	6	£3,564	8	£6,792	11	£9,339	10	£5,940	35	£25,635
7	Casa Luz	5	£2,795	9	£7,191	11	£8,789	6	£3,354	31	£22,129
8	Casa Marco	6	£3,018	9	£6,471	12	£8,628	9	£4,527	36	£22,644
9	Casa Moura	5	£2,725	10	£7,790	12	£9,348	8	£4,360	35	£24,223
10	Chateau Alexa	1	£1,043	7	£10,430	11	£16,390	4	£4,172	23	£32,035
11	Irene	9	£5,409	9	£7,731	12	£10,308	10	£6,010	40	£29,458
12	La Belle Vacance	6	£4,050	9	£8,685	12	£11,580	9	£6,075	36	£30,390
13	La Marina	1	£1,904	6	£16,320	11	£29,920	6	£11,424	24	£59,568
14	Las Palmmares	6	£3,480	9	£7,461	11	£9,119	8	£4,640	34	£24,700
15	Sete Estrelo	6	£3,774	6	£5,394	10	£8,990	8	£5,032	30	£23,190
16	The Vines	7	£4,452	10	£9,090	11	£9,999	11	£6,996	39	£30,537
17	Villa Marlene	7	£3,178	9	£5,841	11	£7,139	7	£3,178	34	£19,336
18	Villa Olivia	11	£6,226	11	£8,899	11	£8,899	11	£6,226	44	£30,250
19	Villa Zivia	3	£3,486	6	£9,960	12	£19,920	5	£5,810	26	£39,176
20									Grand total	533	£461,515

Figure 69 The Summary worksheet

8 Return to the 1st Quarter worksheet and increase the number of weeks reserved by 1, *for each of the villas*. Notice that the Summary worksheet automatically changes.

9 Undo the changes you made at Step 8 and then save your work.

Producing graphs and charts

Graphs and charts can be very helpful tools to illustrate numerical data in a visual format, and spreadsheet programs provide easy-to-use facilities to create the graphs and charts.

Probably the most frequently used examples are

- column charts
- bar charts
- pie charts.

A well-presented graph or chart might include

- a *main title*
- *axis titles* – used on bar and column charts to show what the axes represent
- *data labels* – which can show the actual value or a percentage figure
- a *legend* (sometimes referred to as a *key*) to explain the segments of a pie chart or two or more sets of data in a column or bar chart.

You can see quite clearly in Figure 70 that the 3rd Quarter has the highest number of weeks reserved. However, do you think that Figure 71 might be more useful because it shows the actual values at the end of the bars? Figure 72 shows the value of bookings as a percentage, which indicates that the income in the 3rd Quarter is nearly half of the income for the year. These three charts provide useful graphical representation of different aspects of the data relating to the bookings and income of the villas.

When creating graphs or charts, it is essential to be absolutely clear about what data you wish to illustrate. When you have completed the graph or chart, ask yourself these questions:

- Is the chart style effective?
- Are the titles suitable?
- Do you need axis titles?
- Do you need a legend?

Axis label

Figure 70 Column chart showing the total number of weeks for which villas were reserved each quarter

Data label

Figure 71 Bar chart showing the total value of bookings for each quarter

Legend or key

Figure 72 Pie chart showing the total value of bookings for the year, as percentages per quarter

TiP

When you create spread-sheets for your e-portfolio, it will be an excellent plan to include your own name, the filename and date in the footer. You might want to include other information as well.

Headers and footers

Just as in a word processor, you can include a header or footer in your spreadsheet. In Excel you can choose to have the page number, the sheet name, filename and date inserted automatically.

If the worksheet covers more than one page, the header or footer will automatically appear on all the pages. However, if you have more than one worksheet in your workbook, then you will need to put the footer on all the worksheets.

To insert a footer into a worksheet, select **View**, **Header and Footer** and then **Custom Footer**. The dialogue box shown in Figure 73 will appear.

The filename was automatically inserted in the centre section by clicking on the Excel icon, and the date in the right section by clicking on the date icon. The date will be updated each time you make changes to the file. When the spreadsheet is printed, the actual filename and date will be shown.

Figure 73 Creating a footer in Excel

Printing a spreadsheet

To print from Excel you can either click on the familiar **Print** icon or you can select **File**, **Print** and press **OK**.

However, it is well worth checking **Print Preview** before sending the file to print, to make sure the printout will *look* as you want it. Do remember that with spreadsheets the layout is usually wide, so landscape orientation is more common than portrait.

As with Microsoft Word, through the *Page Setup* dialogue box you can

- change margins
- select portrait or landscape
- include a header or footer.

You can also print the spreadsheet

- with or without gridlines
- with or without row and column headings
- showing the values or the formulas.

Businesses rarely print the row and column headings, but your teacher or tutor may want them included in your coursework, since it makes it easier to check your formulas.

Spreadsheets used in business are often very large – one worksheet in Excel allows you to use hundreds of columns and more than 10,000 rows! We have never used a worksheet that large, and you probably won't either, but even with much smaller worksheets you are likely to want to print just a part of it. Excel allows you to do this very easily.

Jargon buster

The **print area** is the actual part of the worksheet that you want to print. This may mean selecting all the data without any surrounding blank cells. Alternatively it might involve selecting just a part of the worksheet that you wish to print.

Presentation software

Presentations can be in a variety of forms. At school or college your teacher may present information using an overhead projector and slides. A cinema's booking office could use a computer to show a series of pictures about forthcoming films; this would also be a presentation.

Travelbug could use Microsoft PowerPoint to create a presentation of its products and services to show prospective clients. You will probably be asked to deliver a PowerPoint presentation during your school or college studies, and you may even be asked to deliver one when you go for a job interview. Learning to use PowerPoint effectively will therefore provide you with a skill that you will find useful both now and in the future.

LEARNING OUTCOMES

You need to learn about

✓ designing and creating the structure and navigating route of a presentation

✓ selecting and creating colour schemes

✓ creating and using a corporate style

✓ creating and selecting components – text and graphics

✓ using master slides and templates

✓ using frames

✓ editing text – fonts, aligning, bullets and numbering, line spacing

✓ editing graphics – aligning, rotating, flipping, cropping and resizing, changing colour and resolution, optimising file size

✓ adding lines and simple shapes

✓ using text wrap

✓ inserting animation

✓ creating slide transitions

✓ producing speaker notes and handouts to accompany slide shows.

Designing and creating the structure of a presentation

A PowerPoint presentation is made up of individual parts, called *slides*. You can build up a series of slides to create a presentation. Often you will see a PowerPoint presentation displayed through a digital projector on to a screen. You may have experienced your teachers doing this in lessons. Alternatively the presentation could be shown on a computer screen as an on-screen display – for example the presentation about forthcoming films.

It is essential to plan a presentation before creating it. This includes creating a *storyboard* that shows the layout and content of each individual slide. You should also plan the structure of the presentation, making sure you show the *navigation route*. There is an opportunity to learn more about storyboards and structures in Unit 2 of the qualification.

Using wizards, templates and master slides

Wizards

You may already be familiar with the wizards used in applications such as Microsoft Access. PowerPoint also provides a wizard to simplify the creation of a presentation. In PowerPoint this is called the *AutoContent Wizard* (Figure 74). If you want to create a presentation quickly and be guided step by step, this is an ideal feature.

Figure 74 The AutoContent Wizard

Templates

PowerPoint also makes creating a presentation easier by providing a wide range of design and presentation *templates* (Figure 75).

A design template is a file that has been designed with special backgrounds and layouts ready to use. It includes styles for the type and size of bullets and fonts. Using a design template is another timesaving feature, and, if you are not particularly artistic, can be invaluable.

The design template always has two slide designs – one used for the title slide (the first slide in a presentation) and one used for the remaining slides. This means that the title slide will have a slightly different design from the remaining slides in a presentation.

Presentation templates are pre-structured presentations that you can choose to suit a specific purpose (Figure 76). For example, Thomas Tripp from Travelbug could use the marketing plan template to create a presentation to market holidays to prospective clients.

If you don't want to use one of the templates supplied with PowerPoint, you can find different themes and design templates on the Internet, many of which you can download without charge.

Figure 75 The Design Templates window

Figure 76 The Presentation Templates window

The slide master

Each design template comes with a *slide master* on which you can put any graphics or text that you want to appear on every slide, and an optional *title master* where you can make changes to slides in your presentation that use the title slide layout. For example, Travelbug can put their logo on the slide master so that it will appear on every slide (Figure 77).

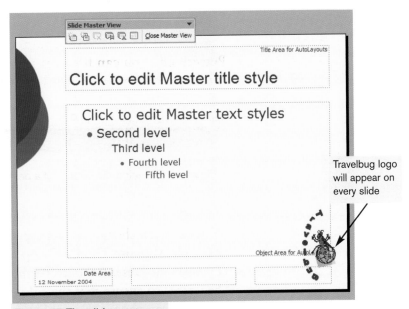

Figure 77 The slide master

If you wish to divide your presentation into several sections, each starting with a title slide, you can create a separate title master. You edit the slide masters and title masters to set the default text formats and styles for all slides in your presentation. You can also number each slide, include a footer, and show the date a presentation was created.

Selecting and creating colour schemes

Colours are used for the background, text and lines, shadows, title text, fills, accents, and hyperlinks on a slide. Together they are called the presentation's *colour scheme*.

If you choose to use an existing template for your presentation, one useful feature is that if you do not like the colour scheme then you can change it easily (Figure 78). A design template will include a default colour scheme for the presentation, together with additional alternative schemes to choose from.

The predetermined colour schemes available with the Eclipse design template

Figure 78 Changing the colours of a design template

You can even change certain aspects of a default colour scheme. For example, suppose Thomas Tripp of Travelbug wants to create a PowerPoint presentation to be shown at a travel exhibition. Because he wishes to ensure that the colour scheme uses the Travelbug house style, he can choose to modify the design template to reflect this. As PowerPoint allows you to change the colour for all or only certain elements of a colour scheme, Thomas Tripp could change the colour for text and lines, but leave the other elements unchanged (Figure 79).

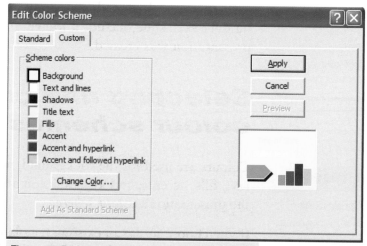

Figure 79 Dialogue box to edit a colour scheme

Colour schemes can be applied to one slide, selected slides or the entire presentation. If you are creating the template yourself for a presentation, you can apply colour schemes in the same way you would if you were using an existing design template.

Viewing your slides

There are three main ways of viewing slides.

- *Normal view*. This is the main view used for editing. It displays three areas. On the left-hand side there are tabs which alternate between slide and outline view, the slide pane and the notes pane. You can adjust the pane sizes by dragging the pane borders. Slides are displayed individually and you can work on the slides in this view. The notes pane allows you to enter notes that you want to make about a slide, which will assist you when making a presentation.

- *Slide sorter*. This allows you to view all the slides in miniature form. Not only can you delete slides, change the order of slides or insert new slides in slide sorter view, you can also copy existing slides and paste them into the desired positions very easily.

- *Slide show*. You can view your presentation by clicking on the Slide Show icon in the bottom-left.

Creating, selecting and using text and graphics components

Slide layout

It is possible to design your own slides from scratch, or to choose one of the layouts provided by PowerPoint. The *Slide Layout* option will display the different layouts from which you can choose. By pointing to each picture you can see a description of the slide.

The layouts are divided into different categories – *Text Layouts*, *Content Layouts*, *Text and Content Layouts*, and *Other Layouts*. Figure 80 shows the different layouts, which allow a range of components to be included in a slide: text (including bulleted lists), charts, graphics, sound and video (referred to as *media clips*).

Figure 80 The slide layout options

PowerPoint allows you to click on icons to add the appropriate content for a slide. For example, Thomas Tripp would click on the **Insert Picture** icon to insert a digital photograph in his presentation (Figure 81).

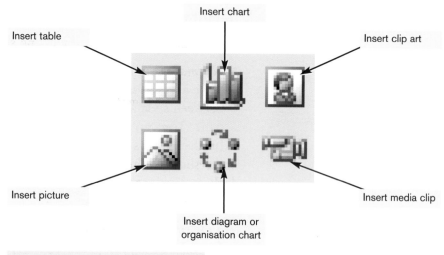

Figure 81 The components available

Using boxes/frames

The design of each slide is broken down into areas called *boxes* (sometimes referred to as *frames*). Each box/frame holds an object. The object can be, for example, a list, a title, text, a piece of clip art, or a chart. A box can be copied, moved and resized in the same way as you would a piece of clip art, and can even be rotated.

You can either use one of the slide layouts provided by PowerPoint, or start with a blank slide and insert objects wherever you like on the slide. These objects are automatically held in boxes.

Editing text on slides

Many of the features that you may be familiar with from using other applications – such as Word or CorelDraw – can be applied to text in PowerPoint by selecting **Format** on the *Standard* toolbar (Figure 82). You can format text to bold, italic, underlined or shadowed, and align text to the left, centre, right or justify it. You can change the colour of text and choose from a wide range of fonts and sizes.

TiP

PowerPoint includes a spellchecker. All Microsoft Office applications use the same dictionary file to check spellings. If you add a word to the dictionary in Word, PowerPoint will also recognise it.

Skills check ▶▶

Refer to page 88 for information on formatting bulleted and numbered lists.

TiP

Take care always to use a font size that can be read easily. Font size 24 or above is a good size to read. Font size 12 or 14 may be fine for a handout, but it would be impossible to read from the back of a room!

Skills check ▶▶

The Artwork and Imaging skills section of this book covers editing techniques which you can use when modifying images for a PowerPoint presentation.

Skills check ▶▶

Positioning, cropping, resizing, grouping and borders are controlled in the same way as in Microsoft Word (page 83).

Figure 82 The Format menu options

Using the *Line Spacing* dialogue box from the **Format** menu, you can adjust the line spacing, not only between lines, but before and after paragraphs, just as you can in Word.

Some slide layouts allow for text areas that are specifically for lists. When you start typing in one of these, a bullet will appear before the text. You can format the bullets to different styles, in the same way as you would in Word. You can also create numbered lists, again exactly as you would in Word.

Editing and using graphics

The graphics you include in a presentation could be a photograph taken with a digital camera, some clip art, a drawing, or perhaps a logo such as the Travelbug logo.

Think it over ...

Have you heard the expression 'a picture is worth a thousand words'? Including graphics in a presentation will ensure that it is more interesting, often easier to understand and – most importantly – more memorable.

You may decide to use a specialist editing package or the *Picture* toolbar in PowerPoint (Figure 83) to edit a graphic. For instance, Thomas Tripp might decide to adjust the colour and resolution of a digital photograph using Coral Photo-Paint or Microsoft Photo Editor rather than use the more limited options supplied with PowerPoint.

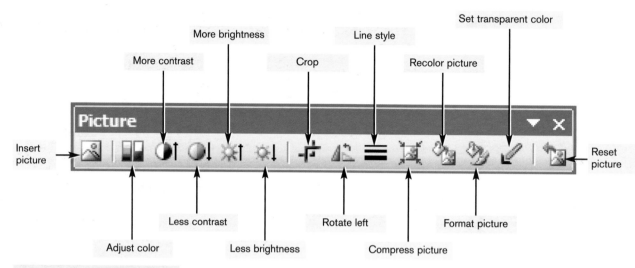

Figure 83 The Picture toolbar

Inserting clip art

Inserting clip art into a slide is very easy – PowerPoint comes with a gallery (Figure 84). If you have an Internet connection, you can click on the **Clips Online** button on the menu bar. This will connect you to Microsoft's database of free clip art. You can also buy a CD-ROM full of pictures you can use.

TiP

*The Internet is a wonderful source of graphics that you can download. However, whatever the source of your graphics, it is important to remember to check that you are allowed to use them. If the creator says that a picture is in the **public domain**, then this means that the copyright on it has been waived and it is free to use. Otherwise you may have to get permission.*

Click here to access Microsoft's Clips Online.

Figure 84 The Microsoft Clip Organizer

Adding more features

Inserting lines and simple shapes

An example of a rotated callout with text inside

12 November 2004

Figure 85 Using a callout

There are many ways to improve a PowerPoint presentation. You can add lines and shapes, fill the shapes with colour, outline them and make them look three-dimensional. The **Autoshapes** button on the *Drawing* toolbar provides a menu of types of shape, each type having its own sub-menu showing all the shapes available. There are over 150 different shapes to choose from!

Callouts are designed to hold text within the shape. They can be simple boxes with lines pointing from them or 'word and thought' balloons (Figure 85). As with other text boxes, you can resize a callout, and rotate and format its text.

Wrapping text

By default, text inside a shape is wrapped so that it does not spill over the border. If you need to turn this setting off, double-click the shape to display the *Format AutoShape* dialogue, and untick the **Word wrap text in AutoShape** option in the *Text Box* tab (see Figure 86).

Click here to turn off word wrap

Figure 86 Turning off text wrapping in an AutoShape

Inserting WordArt

As with other Microsoft Office programs, such as Word and Excel, you can use the *WordArt* tool to create a logo, or to make text more interesting. One very useful feature is that a design you make in one Office application can be used in any of them. Therefore, if you have used WordArt in Word to create a logo, for example, you could use the same logo in a PowerPoint presentation.

Think it over ...

Look at the two sample slides in Figure 87. One of these has WordArt for the text, and the other does not. Which do you think looks more appealing?

WordArt used for text

Normal text

Figure 87 A comparison of WordArt and normal text

TiP

Remember not to try to include too many sounds. Be careful what you choose – you may enjoy listening to heavy metal, but will your audience?

TiP

Remember the copyright issues you have learned about text and images also applies to music and sound files.

Inserting sounds

Sound can enhance a presentation when used carefully. You can use one of the sound clips provided with PowerPoint, record your own sounds, play sounds off a CD to accompany your presentation, or download sounds from the Internet.

You can add sound effects to your animations using **Insert, Movies and Sounds, Sound From File**. If you wish to, you can even record your own commentary. You cannot, however, use a pre-recorded commentary and another form of recorded sound at the same time.

The final enhancement Thomas Tripp makes to his slide for the Cruise Club presentation is to insert sound. He has chosen 'Sailing' sung by by Rod Stewart. On searching the Internet he finds a free midi (sound) file which he can save to his computer and then insert into the presentation.

Navigation between slides

The default navigation route of a PowerPoint presentation is linear. However, the *Action Settings* feature will allow you to link to another slide further on in your presentation, to another PowerPoint presentation, to a file, or even to a website (Figure 88). You can add settings to text or to an object in your presentation.

Figure 88 Dialogue box for action settings

The **AutoShapes** button on the *Drawing* toolbar also includes a number of action buttons which you can include on slides. This feature can be useful when you wish to move to another part of your presentation, or even to another file.

Thomas Tripp has built a slide which gives examples of what Travelbug can offer their customers (Figure 89). He has also used the action settings facility to link to slides in a different part of the presentation (Figure 90).

By clicking here, the presentation moves out of sequence to show the Cruise Club slide.

Figure 89 Slide with links to different parts of the presentation

Figure 90 Adding a hyperlink from slide 4 to slide 9

Finally, Thomas has included an action button which he has set to return to the last slide viewed.

Using animation

PowerPoint has a clever feature that will allow you to make words and pictures on your slides appear and disappear when you want. This is called *animation*. Instead of being visible immediately when the slide appears, the object that you animate – text, a picture, or a piece of clip art for example – comes in afterwards, appearing in a special way.

Animation controls how an object is brought on to the slide. An object can appear automatically, or wait until the user clicks the mouse button before appearing. If you have more than one animated object on a slide you can control the order in which they appear. The object will always end up where you put it when you were designing the slide.

The simplest way to animate your presentation is to use one of the animation schemes that PowerPoint provides. You have a choice from such things as *Appear and Dim* (Figure 91), *Dissolve In*, and *Spin*. PowerPoint lets you preview how the animation of your text and objects will appear for one slide or for the whole presentation.

Our Aim

- To provide a quality travel experience, at the most competitive price.
- To help you find the holiday which is just right for you, whatever the type of holiday it is.
- To offer a personal service which is second to none, from when you walk through the door to make an enquiry, to when your holiday ends.

The text on this slide has been set to dim once the next bullet point appears.

Figure 91 Using animation in a slide

TiP

You will need to experiment to find out how these animations appear on the screen.

For the more adventurous, there is the *Custom Animation* option, which provides more control of your animations. You can use a lot more animation effects, pick the sound that goes with each animation, choose the order in which animations take place, and set the amount of time to wait between animations. You can decide what happens to an object once it appears, such as making it disappear or change colour.

Creating slide transitions

When you are showing a PowerPoint presentation and move from one slide to the next, this is referred to as *slide transition*. When you design a PowerPoint presentation, each slide has a transition associated with it. The transition will tell PowerPoint how to change the display from one slide to the next.

The latest version of PowerPoint offers over 50 different transition styles from which to choose – examples are *cut*, *dissolve* and *wipe right*. If you prefer, you can choose a random transition, so that a different style and direction will be used each time you move on to a new slide.

You can adjust the speed for slide transitions to be slow, medium or fast. Furthermore, you can make the transitions occur on the click of

? Think it over ...

You will have seen examples of transitions all the time, without realising it. For example, a transition happens when you are watching the television and the scene changes from one shot to another.

a mouse or automatically after a set period of time. You can even set up a presentation to show continuously until the **Esc** key is pressed. Thomas Tripp could use this feature for the slide show he wants to show at a travel exhibition.

Producing speaker notes and handouts

Speaker notes

PowerPoint has a facility called *speaker notes*, which allows you to include notes with a slide. This feature gives a text display for each slide. You can add anything you want in these notes (Figure 92). For example, Thomas Tripp of Travelbug can use this facility to give extra details on the different cities shown on the City Breaks slide of his presentation. The slide, together with the notes, can be printed out to give to prospective customers.

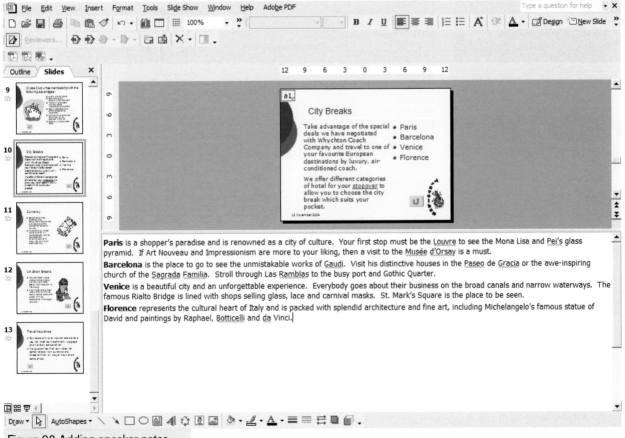

Figure 92 Adding speaker notes

Handouts

Another feature of PowerPoint is that you can print a presentation as a *handout*. You have the option of choosing how many slides per page to print, up to a maximum of nine. If you choose three slides per page, as shown in Figure 93, PowerPoint automatically adds lines to the right-hand side of each slide so that the audience can write their own notes during the presentation.

Figure 93 Options to choose from when printing handouts

Select the Handouts option.

Select number of slides per page.

Shows how the slides will appear when printed.

> ✓ **TiP**
>
> *PowerPoint is a very versatile package, and not all of its features have been discussed in this chapter. You should experiment and learn to use even more of its features.*

> ✓ **TiP**
>
> *It can be tempting to incorporate many different features within a presentation to show off your newly acquired skills. Remember that doing so can distract from the actual content of the presentation!*

Artwork and imaging software

With the power of the modern computer and its ability to select, capture or modify images, you don't have to be an artist to create interesting, imaginative and effective artwork. This book contains a variety of images and artwork: some are screen prints of the computer, some are photographs and some are drawings; some are in black and white and others are in colour. They are all intended to make the book more interesting to read and to help you understand the topics you are studying.

Sometimes a graphical representation can stand alone without any words at all, and at other times the image makes the words much easier to understand, or vice versa. For example, it would be very difficult to describe charts and graphs just in words.

LEARNING OUTCOMES

You need to learn about

✓ selecting and capturing images

✓ modifying images

✓ choosing appropriate resolutions and file formats.

Selecting and capturing images

There are several ways to select and capture images that can then be used to improve the presentation of your e-portfolios. You can select images that are already prepared (such as clip art), create your own using drawing tools, or acquire images electronically by scanning them or downloading photos from a digital camera.

Using clip art and library images

Images can be imported into your documents from libraries on CD–ROM, the Internet, or packaged with the software. Word contains its own selection of images, but far more are available from other sources. Many of these clip art libraries are free.

You can enter a topic in the search field and the computer will find relevant pictures available in the library. A search for 'Australia' produced many results. The search was then refined to show only images first in clip art format and then in photo format. Two images of Sydney Opera House were selected, and copied and pasted into the text for this chapter (Figure 94).

Figure 94 Sydney Opera House in clip art format, and in photo format

Using a scanner

A *scanner* allows you to add pictures from other sources – such as a magazine, book or photograph – into your documents (Figure 95). The scanner reads the information and converts it into digital format.

Figure 95 A scanner

The document is placed inside the scanner. Once the image has been scanned, it can be stored in the computer and used intact or edited as required. The scanned image is stored in picture format, even if it is text – unless text recognition software is available, in which case the text is stored as data that can be edited using a word processor.

Using a digital camera and downloading images

Digital cameras look very similar to traditional cameras (Figure 96), but most of them allow you to view the image on a small liquid-crystal display (LCD) screen built into the camera. As soon as you take a picture, you can view it on the screen and decide whether to keep it or to retake the shot. With a traditional camera the picture is recorded on film, so you have no idea how good or bad the photograph is until the film has been processed.

Figure 96 A digital camera

With a digital camera, light intensities are converted into a digital form that can be stored on a memory card or stick. The images can then be downloaded into the computer, viewed on screen, saved and imported into a document or printed on special photographic-quality paper. The digital images can also be taken to photographic shops and printed in the same size formats as standard photographs taken on film.

Modifying images

Once an image has been captured electronically, it is possible to modify the image to suit your purpose exactly.

Grouping and ungrouping

Several different images can be combined to make a new image. The logo designed for Travelbug (Figure 97) was created using WordArt for the text, combined with two clip art images: the world plus an insect sitting on top!

Once the two images were positioned correctly, they were grouped together using the *Drawing* toolbar (Figure 97). The WordArt was resized, rotated to fit around the image, and the colour of the letters changed to blend in. All three elements of the logo were then grouped together.

Figure 97 WordArt and clip art images are highlighted and grouped to make the logo

When the images have been grouped in this way they can be manipulated as one image. If you then wish to change part of the image, you can click on the image and this time select **Draw, Ungroup** from the *Drawing* toolbar. After the necessary changes have been made, the individual images can be regrouped to make one image. It is much easier to work with a grouped image because all the elements move together and can be resized in proportion.

Cutting, pasting, cropping, trimming and resizing images

Sometimes you find that what you require is part of a bigger picture. For example, the Sydney Opera House scene shown in Figure 94 (page 142) included a lot of water and sky. If you wanted only the actual opera house, you could cut out that section by using the crop (trim) tool to remove the unwanted sections (Figure 98).

Figure 98 Sydney Opera House cropped and resized

Another method of cropping an image is to use the mask tools that are typically available in graphics software.

- The first mask enables you to draw a rectangular shape around the area you wish to keep.
- The second mask enables you to draw a circle around the area you wish to keep.
- The third mask enables you to draw a freehand shape around the area you wish to keep.

Once the area to be kept has been identified, the image can be cropped to the mask.

To obtain the image of these mask tools, a screen print was made showing the toolbars in Corel Photo-Paint (Figure 99). The rectangular mask was used to select the mask icons and, once the image was 'cropped to mask', the rest of the screen print was removed leaving just the three mask tools.

Figure 99 Corel Photo-Paint toolbars

Aligning, rotating, and flipping images

Aligning an image

The **Align or Distribute** options on the *Drawing* toolbar allow you to place an image in a particular position on the page (Figure 100).

Figure 100 The sub-menu to align an image

This facility can be very useful if, for example, you wish to position the image exactly in the middle of the page, which is quite difficult just by dragging the image into position. Click on the image, select **Relative to Page** and then **Align Middle** – the image will be placed in the centre of the page.

When drawing a diagram, you may wish to draw a series of boxes the same size and then arrange them to line up evenly on the page. It can be quite difficult to do this just by dragging the boxes into position (Figure 101). Instead, select the boxes and choose **Draw, Align or Distribute, Align Left** from the *Drawing* toolbar.

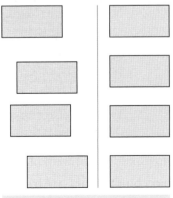

Figure 101 Boxes unaligned, and then aligned and spaced evenly

Figure 102 The AutoShape arrow rotated in various directions

Rotating an image

An image can be rotated to the left, to the right or freely. The *AutoShape arrow* points to the right, but suppose you need an arrow pointing upwards. Select the arrow and rotate left, which changes the direction to point up. If you select free rotate, then the arrow can be angled to any direction you choose (Figure 102).

Flipping an image

If you flip an image, you reverse the direction in which the image is pointing. For example, suppose you need a picture of a horse facing to the right. You have found a good picture but the horse is pointing to the left. You can use the picture and flip it to the right (Figure 103) using **Draw**, **Rotate or Flip**, **Flip Horizontal**.

Figure 103 An image flipped horizontally

You can also flip an image vertically so it turns upside down (Figure 104).

Figure 104 An image flipped vertically

Choosing appropriate image resolutions and file formats

Optimising image resolution for print and digital publications

There are two basic types of images on a computer:

- bitmaps
- vectors.

Bitmaps

A *bitmap* image is made up of dots, whereas a *vector* image is made up of various elements such as lines, curves, circles and squares.

The sharpness or clarity of a bitmap image is determined by its *resolution*, which is measured by the number of *pixels* (or dots) it contains per inch (dpi). A general 'rule of thumb' is to use 72 dpi for on-screen images and up to 300 or 600 dpi for printed images.

Figure 105(a) shows a bitmap image of a bird with a clear resolution. Figure 105(b) shows the same image increased to approximately 3.5 times the original size, and you can see clearly that the resolution has deteriorated. Figure 105(c) shows an enlarged section of the bird's beak. Notice that the edge of the beak is now looking very ragged and uneven. Figure 105(d) shows the same enlargement including the gridlines. The individual pixels are clearly visible, which is very useful if you wish to edit a picture.

TiP

As a bitmap image is enlarged, the quality becomes poorer. There will be a point beyond which the quality is unacceptable for all normal uses.

TiP

If you want to create an image as a bitmap then it is important to design it at the size it should be printed.

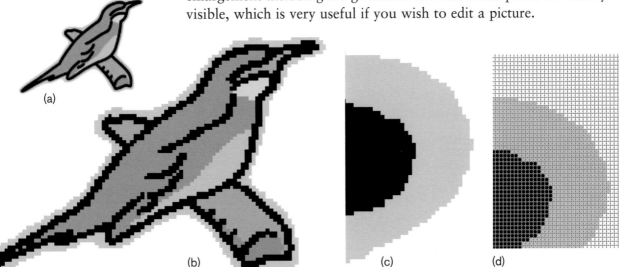

(a)

(b)　(c)　(d)

Figure 105 (a) Bitmap image of a bird. (b) The same image enlarged about 3.5 times. (c) An enlarged section of the beak. (d) An enlarged section of the beak showing the individual pixels and gridlines

Vector graphics

In vector graphics, objects are treated as collections of lines rather than patterns of individual dots. This makes it easier to enlarge the image without reducing its sharpness or quality (Figure 106). However, many people believe that bitmap images provide more subtlety in shading and texture.

Figure 106 A vector image: notice that the enlargement retains the quality

Internet and intranets

In your studies you will need to research information from a wide variety of sources. A huge amount of information can be obtained if you carry out a search on the Internet or an intranet. However, be warned: there are millions of websites on the World Wide Web and, unless you have the skills to carry out an effective search, you may find it difficult to find the exact information you need.

Jargon buster

The **Internet** is the world's largest computer network, connecting millions of organisations and people across the globe.

An **intranet** uses the same technology as the Internet but is an internal communication system for a particular organisation or company. It can be accessed only by authorised users. It allows secure email communication and distribution of data.

The **World Wide Web** is a part of the Internet. Multimedia documents are connected together using **hyperlinks**. Each document is called a **web page** and a set of web pages make up a **website**.

LEARNING OUTCOMES

You need to learn about

✓ using features of browser software

✓ using search engines and portals.

Jargon buster

Broadband is the general term given to the latest in high-speed Internet access technology, which is much faster than using a dial-up modem. An Asymmetric Digital Subscriber Line (ADSL) is an example of always-on broadband technology. It uses an ordinary telephone line to allow you to access the Internet and talk on the telephone at the same time.

Using features of your browser software

The special software which enables you to search the Internet or an intranet is known as a *web browser*. A web browser enables you to view web pages and to click on links – known as *hyperlinks* – to other web pages and websites. The most common web browsers are Microsoft Internet Explorer and Netscape Navigator.

When you double-click on your browser to start it up, you can access web pages only if you are connected to the Internet via your *Internet Service Provider (ISP)*. You may have an 'always on' *broadband connection*, or you may have a 'dial-up' connection (which means that your modem has to dial to your ISP before you can access the Internet).

Jargon buster

A **modem** is a device that converts the digital signals from a computer into analogue signals that can be sent down a phone line. These analogue signals are then converted back to digital signals by a modem at the receiving end.

Jargon buster

A web page has its own unique identification or address known as a **uniform resource locator** (URL). Every address is constructed in the same manner and usually starts with 'http://www'. For example, the web address of the publishers of this book is http://www.heinemann.co.uk (Figure 108).

The home page

When you launch a web browser while connected to the Internet, the default web page – the *home page* – will be loaded and appear on screen. This can be the intranet of the company whose computer you are using, the website of your ISP, or any website you have chosen.

Finding a website

If you know the *website address* (URL) you can go directly to it by typing it in the Address box of the browser and clicking on **Go**. If you don't know the address of a company or organisation, try guessing. It is often possible to guess correctly, as organisations usually try to include their name in the address. You don't even have to type 'http://www' because the browser will add that for you. Figure 107 shows the toolbar and Address box in Internet Explorer.

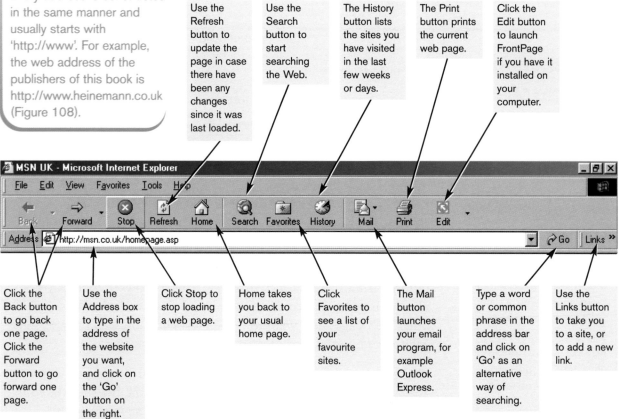

Use the Refresh button to update the page in case there have been any changes since it was last loaded.

Use the Search button to start searching the Web.

The History button lists the sites you have visited in the last few weeks or days.

The Print button prints the current web page.

Click the Edit button to launch FrontPage if you have it installed on your computer.

Click the Back button to go back one page. Click the Forward button to go forward one page.

Use the Address box to type in the address of the website you want, and click on the 'Go' button on the right.

Click Stop to stop loading a web page.

Home takes you back to your usual home page.

Click Favorites to see a list of your favourite sites.

The Mail button launches your email program, for example Outlook Express.

Type a word or common phrase in the address bar and click on 'Go' as an alternative way of searching.

Use the Links button to take you to a site, or to add a new link.

Figure 107 The Internet Explorer toolbar

Protocol: Web URLs begin with 'http' (or 'https' for secure password-protected websites).

Top-level domain (TLD): This combination of letters indicates the type of site. For example, '.co' indicates a company and '.gov' indicates a government department.

http://www .heinemann .co .uk

Figure 108
The Heinemann
URL explained

Server: This is the name of the computer hosting the website. It is usually 'www'.

Domain name: This is where the business name will appear.

Country: This national TLD indicates the country. For example, '.uk' indicates the United Kingdom, 'ie' indicates Ireland, and 'es' indicates Spain.

Top-level domains (TLDs) indicate the type of site. Examples of useful top-level domains to know are listed in Figure 109.

.ac	A university, college or academic department
.co	A company
.com	A commercial organisation
.uk.com	An alternative area for UK registrations, often used if the .com or .co.uk name is not available
.gov	A government department
.me	An individual
.mil	A military site
.net	A network-related site
.org	Generally a charity or non-profit-making organisation
.sch	A school
.tv	The latest domain for television websites

Figure 109 Top-level domains

Hyperlinks within websites

Many companies have very large websites, starting with a home page and panning out with many pages about different aspects of their company. These pages are connected together by hyperlinks. When you move your mouse pointer over a hyperlink, the arrow changes to a pointing hand. When you click on the hyperlink you will be connected to this link.

It is very easy sometimes to get lost within a company's website, but a well constructed site will always have a link that takes you to the home page. There will usually be hyperlinks to return you back to the top of a page and to the other main areas of the site. Figure 110 shows some examples of hyperlinks.

Jargon buster

A **hyperlink** is a link on a web page or document which, when you click on it, opens another web page within a website, a different website or a file. Hyperlinks are usually underlined and in another colour, but can also be graphics.

Television

• Pick: **Himalaya with Michael Palin**
9pm **BBC One**

• BBC TV schedules

Popular programmes:
EastEnders | Smile | TOTP | Lottery

Figure 110 Hyperlinks

Large organisations, such as the BBC, will usually include a search facility for their own site, so that you can quickly find the information you require. The BBC's site even has a 'search help and tips' page to help you find the information easily. This is a good website to bookmark in your favourites – you will find a host of useful resources to help you with your studies.

Jargon buster

Internet Explorer calls bookmarks **favorites** (spelt the American way).

✓ TiP

If you share a machine with several people, it is a good idea to create a folder for each person. You can then keep your own favourites separate and easy to find.

Bookmarks

In the same way as you can put a bookmark in a book to return to a page quickly and easily, you can bookmark your favourite websites. You can create folders in which to file these bookmarks, in the same way as you organise and save your files on your hard drive.

Rather than having to remember the address of a website, you can easily return to a site by selecting the name from the favourites list. If there is a specific page within a website that you know you will want to return to on other occasions, you can bookmark that page, rather than the home page of the site.

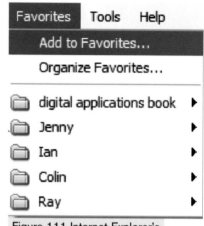

Figure 111 Internet Explorer's Favorites folder

By using the **Organize Favorites** option, you can add, rename and delete folders. You can also change the order in which you view your favourites so that websites that you visit on a regular basis appear higher in the list.

✓ TiP

Caching pages will save a lot of time and money if you are paying for online time.

The Back and Forward buttons

All the time you are online, your browser is storing copies of the pages you have recently used in a memory area called *cache*. If you wish to return to a page you visited before, click on **Back** until you reach the page you require. Because the browser program does not have to go back to the Internet, but simply has to look into its internal cache, the page will appear more quickly than it did the first time. You can click on the **Forward** button to return to the web page you were on before you clicked **Back**.

The Refresh button

When you use the **Back** and **Forward** buttons, any changes that may have occurred since you first visited the relevant page will not appear, because the browser has not gone back to the online web page but has merely loaded that page from its internal cache. Clicking on the **Refresh** button will update the page in case there have been any changes since it was last loaded.

For example, by visiting the British Airports Authority plc's (BAA plc) website through www.heinemann.co.uk/hotlinks (express code 9850P), it is possible to check when flights have landed. When you first visit the site, the flight may be shown with its expected arrival time (Figure 112). By clicking on the **Refresh** button at regular intervals you will be able to check when it has actually landed.

Figure 112 The BAA website, which is being constantly updated with flight information

TiP

Selecting a site from the history list is a quick way of returning to it.

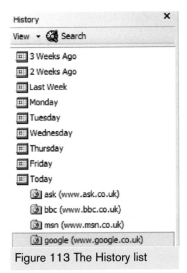

Figure 113 The History list

History

Your browser will store a history of all the websites you have visited over the last few days or weeks. This can be helpful if you have forgotten to bookmark a particularly useful site. It is also useful if you have been surfing the net for some time, and you want to return to a page that you previously visited during the current session.

One way to go back to the page is to click the **Back** button, but this can be quite slow if you have visited a few pages. Another way is to use the *History* list to select the site (Figure 113).

TiP

Do remember when you save or copy text from web pages to take into account the copyright issues (see page 78). Some web developers protect their pages so that images and web pages cannot be copied (see Figure 114).

Figure 114 Example of a copyright message

Copying and saving web pages

You can copy text from a website and paste it into another document using the same techniques as you would in Word or Excel. You can also save whole web pages and images from a website on to your computer.

When you save a web page it will be saved in *HTML* (hypertext mark-up language – see page 170). Once you have saved a web page, you can view it through your browser even when you are offline.

Selecting and printing pages

It is also possible to print web pages that you wish to keep for future reference. Many web pages, such as the one shown in Figure 115, include their own Print hyperlink. However, you can also print a page by selecting **File, Print** from the menu in the usual way.

The selected text can be printed.

Click here to print the whole page in a printer-friendly format.

Figure 115 Selecting text to be printed from a web page

Sometimes when you print a web page you find that the material on the right-hand side is cut off. If this happens you will need to change the orientation of the page to landscape using **File, Page Setup** from the menu. You will have practised these skills already with a word processor.

If you want to print a small section of the page, again you can use the skills you have already learned when using other applications such as Word. Select the text you want to print (see Figure 115) and then choose **File, Print** and click on **Selection** before pressing **OK**.

The Go button

You can use the **Go** button on the Address bar to search for web pages. If you type a common name or word in the address bar and click on **Go**, Internet Explorer will either automatically display the web page or list those that are the most likely match.

For example, if you type 'virgin trains' in the Address bar and click on **Go** you will automatically be directed to the Virgin Trains website. However, if you type 'record shops' in the Address bar, a list of possible web pages will be displayed.

Jargon buster

A **portal** is a website that offers news, weather information or other services, set up as an entry point to the Web. Most portals are also search engines.

Using search engines

The Internet is the world's largest source of information. However, as you have probably already discovered, there are millions of websites, so it is sometimes quite hard to find the information you want.

If you want to find a particular company, or a certain piece of information, you will need to use a *search tool*. There are several different search tools, the main types being search engines, subject directories, meta-searches and name directories. Figure 116 explains what these are.

You might well be thinking that not only is there a huge amount of information to search, but also many different ways of searching, and you would be right! Choose one search tool and just use that one for a while. If you are not sure which one to choose, ask your friends or your teacher or tutor. When you are used to how it works and what sort of results you get then try another search tool.

- **Search engines** are indexes that work by keywords and context. Popular search engines include Altavista, Ask Jeeves and Google (see www.heinemann.co.uk/hotlinks (express code 9850P) for more). Search engines use a program called a *spider*, *robot* or *crawler* to index huge collections of Internet files. Use search engines when you want to find large numbers of related documents or specific types of document such as image files, MP3 music files or discussion lists.

- **Subject directories** are similar to search engines, but are smaller collections of Internet files grouped by subject headings. These files are not found by software, but chosen by humans. These directories are ideal if you wish to research a general topic and you want to avoid all the irrelevant files that search engines can find. An example of a search directory is Open Directory Project (see www.heinemann.co.uk/hotlinks (express code 9850P) for more).

- **Meta-search engines** send searches to several search engines at the same time. Within a few seconds, you get back results from all the search engines that were queried. Meta-search engines do not own a database of web pages; they send your search terms to the databases maintained for other search engines. You can download and install a meta-search engine to work alongside your browser. Copernic is an example of a meta-search engine which can be downloaded (see www.heinemann.co.uk/hotlinks (express code 9850P) for more). Use meta-searches when you want to get an overall picture of what the Internet has on your topic and to check whether the Internet really is the best place for you to search.

- **Name directories** such as Yell (see www.heinemann.co.uk/hotlinks (express code 9850P) for more) are used when you want to search for people by name, telephone number, email address, postcode and so on.

Figure 116 Search tools

Successful searching

As mentioned earlier, sometimes searching can be difficult because, if you do not narrow your search in some way, you can be presented with a large number of irrelevant results. There are ways to overcome this, but these differ between search engines: look at their help pages for tips. Check out the number of hits a search produces, and, if necessary, refine your search to limit the number.

Imagine you are searching for a holiday villa to rent in the Dordogne region of France.

- If you entered *holidays* in the search box of a search engine this would be an example of a *single-criterion search*. It is important to choose the words you are searching on very carefully in order to reduce the number of results you are likely to get. This simple search produced more than 21 million results in Google, so it is unlikely that you would find the ideal holiday from using it!

- You could try typing the words *holiday villas to rent*. This *refined search* narrowed the number of hits to 668 000.

- You could reduce the number of hits further by putting double quotations marks before and after the search words. You will get more accurate information by doing so. This will find websites that include the exact phrase "*holiday villas to rent*" rather than any websites that include *any of the words in any order*. This search reduced the number of hits to 12 700.

- You can limit the number of hits further by using the + sign to show that the word must appear in the results. Typing "*holiday villas to rent*" +*France* reduced the number of hits to 4470. This is an example of *multiple criteria*, the first criterion being "*holidays villas to rent*" and the second being *France*.

- Some of the results included holiday villas in other countries, so typing "*holiday villas to rent*" +*France* –*Spain* will exclude all sites that have the word *Spain*. This reduced the number of hits to 1560.

- Finally, adding +*Dordogne* to the search, so that it became "*holiday villas to rent*" +*Dordogne* +*France* –*Spain* reduced the number of hits to 889.

Using wildcards

To make sure that you do not miss a good website by using the wrong words in your search, you can use *wildcard* matches.

You can use right-hand or left-hand wildcard searches. Entering *water** would produce results that include terms such as 'waterside' and 'waterfront'. Entering **bus* would produce results that include terms such as 'bus', 'minibus' and 'trolleybus'.

Figure 117 is a summary of search techniques.

TiP

Google only supports wildcards when searching for missing words in phrases. For example, "holidays in * France" *will find holidays in Paris, France and holidays in rural South-West France.*

- **Single-criterion searches** – single word searches or words grouped together by the use of quotes.
- **Multiple-criterion searches** – multiple word searches that are not grouped together by the use of quotes, or searches that are refined by using logical operators (+ or –).
- **Wildcards** – some search engines (but not Google) allow the use of * as a wildcard. For example, entering *villa** will search for sites including the words 'villa' and 'villas'.

Figure 117 Summary of search techniques

Logical operators

The earlier example of searching for holidays used two logical operators: + and –. Those and other operators are explained further in Figure 118.

Operator	What is does when used in a search	Example	What it means when used in a search
+ (AND)	Place this in front when you want a word to be present in the results of your search.	+Dordogne +France	The words *Dordogne* and *France* must appear somewhere in the results.
– (NOT)	Place this in front when you want to exclude a word from the results of your search.	+Dordogne +France –Spain	The words *Dordogne* and *France* must appear somewhere in the results, but all pages also with *Spain* should be excluded.
OR	Use this when you want either word to be included in the result.	France OR Spain	Web pages are included in the results if either or both search terms appear.
" "	Use this when you want the words to appear together in the same order.	"Holiday villas to rent"	The words must appear in this order.

Figure 118 The principal logical operators you will need to refine searches

TiP

Google also allows you to find synonyms (words with similar meanings) using the tilde (~) character. For example, searching for ~hotel will also return results containing the words inn, accommodation, hoteles *(Spanish) and so on.*

It is important to remember that different search engines will produce different results, so it is a useful exercise to compare the results achieved from different search engines. Most search engines will have an advanced search option which will prompt you to refine your search (Figure 119).

Also, some search engines, like Ask Jeeves, will allow you to type in direct questions. For example, you could type in *Where can I find information about holiday villas to rent in the Dordogne region of France?*

Figure 119 The Google advanced search tool

A warning!

There is no single person or organisation controlling the information that is published on the Internet. This means that the information you find may not always be correct. It may appear convincing and correct but, in fact, be completely wrong or at least misleading. Protect yourself from inaccurate information in these ways:

- Check whether there is a date on the site, and when it was last updated.
- Look to see whether it is possible to contact the site's developer. Is there an email address to contact?
- Try to work out (or at least be aware of) whether the site was developed by someone or some organisation that wants to put across its message – for example a political (sometimes an extreme political) view.

Email

You will probably have used email at school and often at home. When you start your first job after school or college, or if you go on work experience, you will find that email plays an extremely important role in business and few businesses would be able to function without it.

An email is like an electronic letter, sent in most instances via a computer instead of the postal service. Email is a very sophisticated method of electronic transfer, where messages and documents can be sent from one computer to another using a communications link such as a modem and a telephone line. You can receive and send the electronic equivalent of letters, pictures and sounds, and if you have a webcam attached to your PC you can even send a video email.

Documents prepared on a word processor or other software package, or a document scanned into the computer, can be attached to an email.

LEARNING OUTCOMES

You need to learn about

✓ receiving an email

✓ sending an email

✓ using folders to store and organise emails and attachments

✓ **setting the priority of an email**

✓ **setting up and using an email address book**

✓ **setting up and using distribution lists.**

Hardware and software requirements

To send or receive emails you need

- access to a computer
- a phone line
- a modem (an *analogue modem* if you are using an ordinary phone line, or a *broadband modem* if you have an ADSL line)
- an account with an Internet Service Provider (ISP)
- email communication software, such as Microsoft Outlook Express.

Many businesses use more powerful email programs, such as Microsoft Outlook or Lotus Notes.

The ISP will provide an *email account*, a *password* and a *mailbox* on their server. You will be given an *email address*. The address is a short code, often made up of the user's name, followed by the ISP's domain name – but this can vary. In the example in Figure 120 you will see that three email addresses have been used.

ISP = AOL

ISP = BTInternet

ISP = Freeserve

Text box

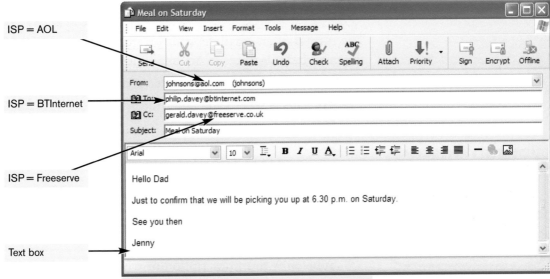

Figure 120 Three ISPs represented in this email

When you are connected to the Internet, you can send your email to the ISP's server. From there it is transmitted to the recipient of the message via another server, this time run by the recipient's ISP. It is stored on that server in a *mailbox* until the person you have emailed logs on to check whether he or she has received any new messages.

Many companies have internal email systems so that all their employees can communicate easily with each other. In this case their email address will usually reflect the company name. For example, Thomas Tripp at the Travelbug travel agency has the email address *Thomas.Tripp@travelbugonline.co.uk*.

You may find that the email address of your school or college includes its name (possibly abbreviated) followed by '.ac.uk'. The '.ac' indicates that you are using an academic network that links all colleges and universities in the UK.

Many people have their own web-based email address through companies such as Hotmail (see www.heinemann.co.uk/hotlinks (express code 9850P) for more). By logging on to the Hotmail website and entering a user name and password, you can access your email wherever you are in the world. Also, more and more ISP's will allow you to log on to the same email account that you usually use at home to check your email using any computer with Internet access.

Sending an email

The format of an email depends on the program you are using, but the most basic features of an email message include the following:

- **From:** This is where you enter your own email address.
- **To:** This is where you enter the address of the recipient of the email.
- **Cc:** This is where you enter the address of someone else who you would like to receive a copy of the e-mail.
- **Bcc:** This is where you enter the address of someone else who you would like to receive a copy of the e-mail *without the other recipients knowing that this copy has been sent* (the B stands for 'blind').
- **Subject:** A short description of what your email is about.
- A text box for the body of the message.

This is demonstrated in Figure 121, which shows an email message ready to be sent.

To send an email using software such as Outlook Express, you would do the following.

- Prepare your message offline (to save on telephone charges, unless you have an always-on connection).
- Click on the **Send** button to store it in the *Outbox* (containing outgoing mail).
- Connect to the Internet via your ISP.
- Click on the **Send and Receive** option.
- You may have to enter a password to access your mailbox at your ISP's server. In Outlook Express and most other programs you can configure the software to store and automatically enter the password.

Jargon buster

'**Cc**' means **carbon copy** and is an expression from the days when carbon paper was used to make copies.

Attach button

Click on Send to store the email in the Outbox.

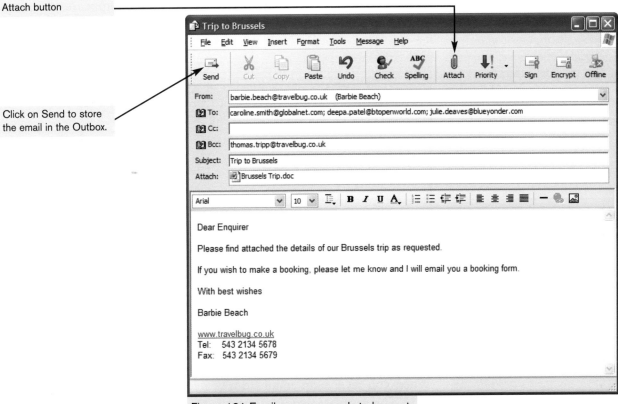

Figure 121 Email message ready to be sent

Your email will be sent to the server at your ISP, and from there to the recipient's ISP.

Sending an email to a group of people

In Figure 121 there are several email addresses in the 'To:' line. Email software will allow you to send emails to more than one person at the same time. In the example, Barbie Beach wants to send details of the Brussels trip to three prospective clients. Note that the email addresses are separated by semicolons (;). You can also Cc or Bcc more than one person in the same way.

Sending an attachment

The **Attach** button allows you to attach (i.e. to send with your email) copies of files stored on your computer. The files can be text, sound, graphics, or even video. In the example in Figure 121, a Word document – Brussels Trip.doc – has been attached.

When you click the **Attach** button, a dialogue box appears, allowing you to locate the file you want to attach (Figure 122).

Figure 122 Adding an attachment

Replying to emails

When you receive an email from someone, you might want to reply to it. The simplest way to do this is to click on the **Reply** button (Figure 123). Alternatively, by clicking on the **Reply All** option, your reply could be sent to both the sender and the other recipients of the email – in this case, Molly Wishhusen. In addition, there is usually the option to forward the email on to someone else.

Figure 123 The Reply and Reply All buttons

When replying to an email, you can choose whether or not to include the original message. Most email software packages will let you set up your system so that the original email is automatically included when you click on the **Reply** button.

Storing and organising emails and attachments

Using folders

It is important to create folders to help organise your emails, in the same way as you manage any other files such as word-processed documents. Most email software will allow you to create folders and sub-folders to help you organise your emails.

In Figure 124 a new folder called 'Using the Internet' is being created as a sub-folder in the 'digital applications' folder.

Once a folder has been created, you can transfer any emails to it by clicking on the message in the message list and dragging it to the folder, as shown in Figure 125.

Figure 124 Creating a folder

 TiP

The more emails you send and receive, the harder it can be to find them. It is good practice to spend some time each week deleting emails that are out of date – for example, an email sent to you by a friend reminding you of a music concert, the date for which has now passed.

Figure 125 Dragging and dropping to organise emails into folders

To make it easier to locate emails, folders can be sorted by date, name of the sender, or subject. If you sort a folder by sender, you can easily find all the messages from one particular person.

Figure 126 Saving an attachment

It is possible to set up rules to automatically store received emails directly into folders *at the time they are received*. This means that your Inbox remains tidy, and emails are easy to find.

When you receive an email with an attachment, it is good practice to save the attachment to a folder in the directory where you keep all such files. This folder could be in your user area if you are at school or college, or it could be in *My Documents* on your home computer. In Figure 126 the Edexcel specification is being saved to the folder 'digital applications book'.

Using a drafts folder

If you wish to prepare an email to send sometime later, most email software packages allow you to save it. For example, in Outlook Express you can save to the Drafts folder by selecting **File, Save** (Figure 127). This will allow you to review the content of the email and send it when you are ready to do so.

Figure 127 Saving a draft email

Setting the priority of an email

Outlook Express and other email software will allow you to set the priority of an email (Figure 128). Emails sent as High Priority can usually be identified by a red exclamation mark.

Figure 128 Choosing the priority of an email

The default setting in Outlook Express is Normal Priority, and there is also the option to send emails as Low Priority. Low Priority emails are identified by a blue down arrow.

The priority you choose for an email will *not* affect its speed of transmission over an internal email system or the Internet.

Setting up and using an email address book

You may have noticed that the To:, Cc: and Bcc: options each have an address button. Clicking any of these buttons takes you to your professional and personal address books.

Setting up an email address book will save you time, as you do not have to try to remember the addresses of email contacts. Your address book will save you having to key in someone's full address every time you send him or her a message. Another advantage of address books is that they help to prevent you from making mistakes, such as a wrong spelling or putting the dot in the wrong place, which would mean your email being returned ('bounced') or delivered to the wrong person.

Most email software, such as Outlook Express, will allow you to save all the details regarding your contacts, including their name, address, email address and phone number (Figure 129).

Outlook Express will also allow you to record other useful information regarding your email contacts, including personal details such as their birthday and even the names of their children.

Jargon buster

An **email contact** is a person or organisation whose details, including name and email address, you have recorded in your email software address book.

Figure 129 The address book entry for one contact

Another feature is that you can give a contact a 'nickname'. In Figure 129 you can see that the nickname given to the email contact is 'IanJ'. This means that if you wanted to send an email you could enter the nickname in the 'To:' line as an alternative to opening the address book, and Outlook Express would automatically retrieve the full email address.

Go out and try!

Add the details of five of your friends to your email address book on the email system you use at school or college. Give each new email contact an appropriate nickname. Send an email to the five contacts confirming that they have been successfully added to your address book.

Open your 'Email' file. Create a new bold heading '**E Activity 4.1**' and write a short paragraph describing the skills you have demonstrated in this activity. Save the file.

Setting up and using distribution lists

A *distribution list* will allow you to send an email to several email contacts simultaneously, but without having to type all the email addresses in the 'To:' box, separated by semicolons.

For example, if Thomas Tripp of the Travelbug agency has decided to send an electronic newsletter to all customers on a monthly basis, it would be extremely tedious for him to have to type in all of the addresses each time the newsletter is sent. It would be sensible for Thomas, in this instance, to set up a distribution list (Figure 130).

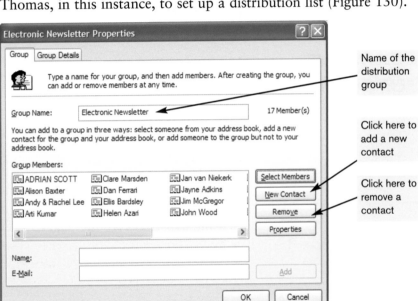

Figure 130 Setting up a group in Outlook Express

Go out and try!

Set up a distribution list (group) called 'Friends' and add the email addresses of the five friends you added to your address book in the last activity. Add the email address of another friend, whose email address you have not as yet added to your address book. Send an email to the distribution group informing them that you have created the new group.

Open your 'Email' file. Create a new bold heading '**E Activity 4.2**' and write a short paragraph describing the skills you have demonstrated in setting up a distribution group for this activity. Save the file.

Web authoring software

Most organisations and businesses would benefit from having a website. The Internet is an extremely good way of advertising goods and services, and many websites allow customers to order goods online. The Travelbug travel agency have decided that it is very important for them to have their own website to promote their business. They will be designing one using Microsoft FrontPage, a very popular website authoring application. This chapter will follow in detail the construction of their site.

LEARNING OUTCOMES

You need to learn about

✓ creating simple web pages

✓ using colour schemes

✓ creating and modifying tables

✓ editing text

✓ editing graphics

✓ adding lines and simple shapes

✓ using hyperlinks to link pages

✓ using text wrapping

✓ using animation options.

Before we consider website authoring software, it is important to understand what a website actually is.

HTML (hypertext markup language)

A *website* is a collection of related web pages. A *web page* is an electronic document that can contain text, images, forms, graphics, and other multimedia elements such as animation. Web pages are created with computer code known as *hypertext markup language* (*HTML*) and then viewed via web browsers, such as Internet Explorer and Netscape.

HTML is in the form of *tags*, which are used around blocks of text to indicate how the text should appear on the screen. The author of a web page designs the page and links all the material together using HTML. When the page is viewed (either by the author or someone viewing a published web page), the web browser software interprets the HTML language and displays the text exactly as the author intended.

HTML enables you to create *hyperlinks* within the text. When the viewer clicks on a hyperlink with a mouse, he or she is taken automatically to another part of the page or to another page on the Internet. A hyperlink might be represented by a word, a button or a picture.

Requirements for creating a simple web page

Most modern word processors enable you to produce HTML pages without the need to understand the coding. You can also use *web authoring tools*, such as Microsoft's FrontPage or Macromedia's Dreamweaver. We shall be looking at this method of creating web pages later in this chapter. However, it is important to know the basic concepts of HTML, so we shall first be looking at how Travelbug can create a web page manually.

In order to create a web page, Travelbug will need at the very least a simple text editor (like Notepad) to write the HTML. Alternatively, a dedicated HTML text editor (such as Allaire's HomeSite) could be used. There are many alternatives that they could use, including dedicated authoring tools. They could also use standard application software such Microsoft Word, which includes a 'Save as HTML' option. There are also many online wizards that will guide you step-by-step through the process of creating a web page – many ISPs offer online tools, for example.

Travelbug also needs at least one web browser – a dedicated software application that will enable them to view their own web pages as they are written.

Although it is possible to rely on a web authoring tool to create web pages, it is a good idea to learn the codes (or tags) used to format and structure the text.

Finally, and perhaps most importantly, good design and presentation skills are required.

TiP

Figure 131 (on page 172) gives a list of common HTML tags.

TiP

Word processors such as Microsoft Word are less effective for writing HTML than basic tools such as Notepad. This is because advanced word processors tend to add extra formatting that interferes with the HTML coding.

HTML tags

When you viewed the source code, did you notice words or letters inside the < and > marks? These are known as 'tags' and are the way the web browser knows how to display the document. For example, tags tell the web browser where to start a new paragraph or print a line of text.

Tags usually come in pairs, with the second tag of the pair beginning with a slash symbol (/) to show that the effect of the first tag should now stop. As an example, the **<h1>** and **</h1>** tags indicate where a main heading begins and ends.

The first tag of any document is **<html>**, which tells the web browser that you a beginning a page of information written in HTML. The closing tag **</html>** is put at the end of the document. Figure 131 lists some other very common tags.

Tag		What it does
<html>	**</html>**	Indicates the beginning and the end of an HTML page.
<head>	**</head>**	The head section of the web page.
<title>	**</title>**	The text that will appear on the title bar.
<body>	**</body>**	All the text in the document is between these tags.
<h1>	**</h1>**	Inserts a heading in the largest font. Other sizes are h2, h3, h4, h5 and h6, which is the smallest.
****	****	Displays characters in bold.
<i>	**</i>**	Displays characters in italics.
<center>	**</center>**	Everything between these tags is centred.
** **		Inserts a line break.
<p>	**</p>**	The text between these tags is treated as a separate paragraph.

Figure 131 Common HTML tags

Not all tags come in pairs. The **
** tag, used to create a line break, comes on its own. The **</p>** tag (end of paragraph) is optional, but it is good practice to include it.

Comment tags

If you want to write something in your HTML page that you don't want to appear on your web page, you use a *comment tag*. The tag that turns the comment on is **<!--** and the tag that turns the comment off is **-->**.

Structure of an HTML document

There are always two parts of an HTML document – the *head* and the *body*.

- The first part of any document is always the head. Information in the head is enclosed between the **<head>** and **</head>** tags. Elements in the head area are not displayed in the web page. The most common element is the document's title, bracketed by the **<title>** and **</title>** tags.

- The body of the document begins after the head and is enclosed within the **<body>** and **</body>** tags. The body will contain all the parts of the web page displayed in a web browser's viewing window.

Colour of the background and fonts

You can include between the **<body>** and **</body>** tags different attributes for the style of the text or the background on the web page.

There are 16 colour names that you can choose from (Figure 132). There are also many different combinations of colours that you can achieve by typing what are called alphanumeric codes. Examples of these are **#FFFFCC** for a pale weak yellow, and **#CCCCFF** for a pale weak blue.

Black	Silver	Green	Lime
Gray*	Olive	Yellow	White
Maroon	Navy	Red	Blue
Purple	Teal	Fuchsia	Aqua

Figure 132 Colour names that can be included in HTML code   *Note the American spelling

Font type and size

Standard headings come in sizes from H1 (the biggest) to H6 (the smallest). It is possible also to choose the font size of standard text. The default size is 3, but using the tag **<font size=4>** will increase the font size.

The default font type in Internet Explorer is *Times New Roman*. By using the tag **<font face=arial>** the font on the web page can be changed to Arial, which is a very popular sans serif font.

Although it is important to understand how to create web pages manually, it is usually quicker to use web-authoring software. The remainder of this unit will show you how to use the features of Microsoft FrontPage to develop web pages.

Establishing the structure of a website

Before you begin creating pages for a multiple-page website, it is important to plan on paper how you want the site to appear. In the same way as when you plan a presentation, you should plan the structure of a website which clearly shows the *navigation route*, and create a *storyboard* that shows the layout and content of each page. A well-designed website will have a clear structure and be easy to navigate.

Using wizards

Most authoring tools will include wizards to make designing a website or web page an easier process. Even a beginner can create a professional looking site by following one of the wizards provided. A wizard will take you step by step through the process, giving you options from which to choose at each stage.

For example, as you can see from Figure 133, the *New Web Site* wizard in FrontPage provides a range of different designs from which to choose. Furthermore, you can create the folder in which to save the *web* at the same time.

Thomas Tripp of Travelbug could decide to use the *Personal Web* wizard in FrontPage to create a website for the company. This wizard will automatically create a basic website with a home page and several pages that link to the home page. The structure will not necessarily be the same as his paper design, but Thomas will be able to amend it very easily. In *Navigation view* it is possible to add or delete pages and rename existing pages.

Figure 134 shows the navigational structure of the Travelbug website with the pages renamed to meet Thomas's needs. It is the construction of this website that you will be following throughout the remainder of this chapter.

Figure 133 FrontPage's New Web Site wizard

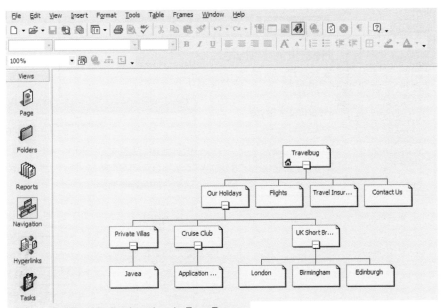

Figure 134 The Navigation view in FrontPage

The next step will be for Thomas to build each web page in turn. However, unlike when a website is coded from scratch in HTML, screen prompts are given on how to continue.

Using colour schemes

Using the themes supplied with FrontPage allows you to create a consistent website. You can either use the colour schemes as they are or make changes that will be reflected on individual pages or throughout the entire website.

If you prefer not to use one of the themes supplied, you can still easily change the background colour, or even include a graphic, by selecting the **Background** option from the **Format** menu.

Also, you can change the text styles used, either in a theme or in a web page you are designing without a theme. For example, if Thomas Tripp decides to change the font style and size for normal text on his website (called 'Body' text), he can click on the **Text** button of the *Themes* dialogue box to do so (Figure 135).

Click here to format theme text

Figure 135 Changing font styles

Using and editing text

Whether you have decided to build a web page from scratch, or to use one of the templates supplied with FrontPage, you will need to add text. One of the benefits of using a web-authoring tool is that you do not need to use HTML to add text. You simply enter the text you want and format it using the normal formatting tools, just as you would in Word. As you are doing this, FrontPage is creating the HTML for you.

Once you have keyed in your text, changing the font type, size and colour is far easier than in HTML. Simply select the text and change the font type, size and colour, just as you would do in Word. You can create bulleted lists and change paragraph formatting – justification and line spacing – again, just as you would do in Word. In FrontPage you can choose the option you require from the **Format** menu (Figure 136).

Skills check ▷▷

See page 86 for a reminder of how to format text in Word.

Figure 136 The Format menu in FrontPage

Figure 137 shows FrontPage dialogue boxes used to format text. You will see that they are very similar to those used in other packages – just remember to select the text first before applying the different formatting.

Figure 137 Dialogue boxes used to format fonts, paragraphs and bullets in FrontPage

Figure 138 shows a possible home page for Travelbug's website, which is still under construction. There are three view buttons – **Normal, HTML** and **Preview**. Use **Normal** view to edit the page, **HTML** view to view or edit the HTML code, or **Preview** view to see how the page will look in a web browser.

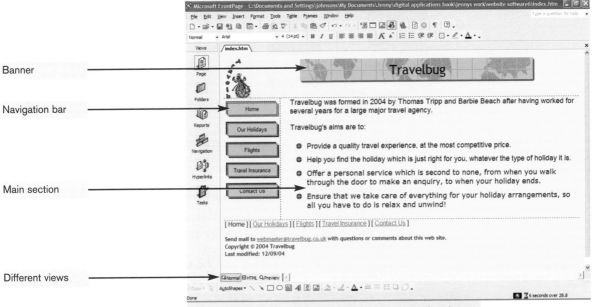

Banner

Navigation bar

Main section

Different views

Figure 138 Travelbug's home page begins to take shape

Page Banner refers to the text and graphic that goes across the top of each page, as in Figure 138. The banner graphic remains the same but the text heading changes on each page. This would be quite a complex task to code using HTML alone, but by using FrontPage the process is extremely simple.

Creating and modifying tables

You have probably guessed by now that if you want to include a table in a web page, it will be more complicated if you do so by writing HTML code than by using FrontPage.

Many of the skills you have learned for creating a table in Word can be applied to FrontPage. You can create a basic structure by using the **Table** menu on the *Standard* toolbar, and then add text or graphics in the cells (Figure 139). You can even include tables within tables! You can merge cells, change their height and width, and apply different borders just as you would in Word.

Skills check ▷▷

See page 96 for a reminder of how to format tables in Word.

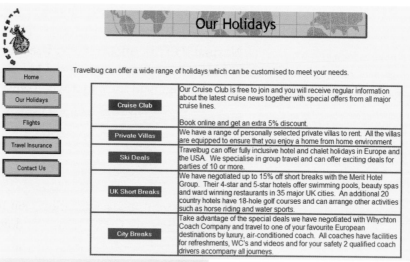

Figure 139 A table created in FrontPage

You can create more complex tables by selecting **Table, Draw Table** from the menu. Once you have drawn a table, you can erase rows and columns from it using the eraser tool.

Tables can be used for arranging information in rows and colums, or for displaying text and graphics on a page. In fact, tables are extremely useful for designing a web page layout. Often tables are used for some or all of a page's layout, although you may not be aware of this when looking at a web page (Figure 140).

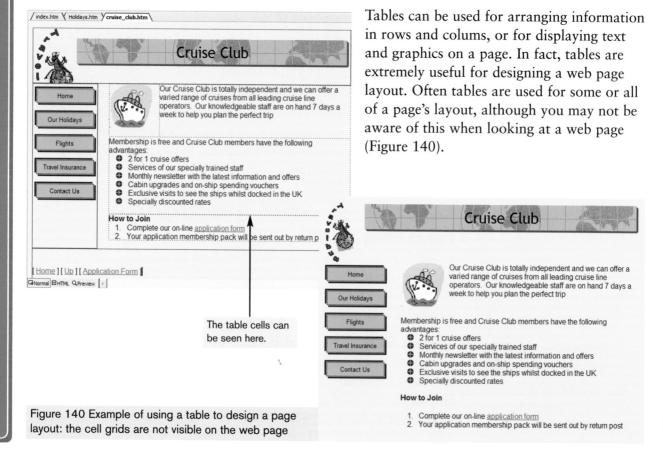

The table cells can be seen here.

Figure 140 Example of using a table to design a page layout: the cell grids are not visible on the web page

Using and editing graphics

Graphics are an important part of any website as they can communicate a lot of information very easily. It is a simple process to insert a graphic into a website being created in FrontPage.

Sourcing the images

The graphics can come from a number of sources, which you will have already learned about in the chapter on artwork and imaging software (page 141).

- Graphics applications allow you to create your own pictures. Examples are CorelDraw, Windows Paint and Adobe Photoshop.
- Clip art is available from various sources.
- You can scan existing photographs or pictures to put into your work.
- Digital still and video cameras allow you to take photos and videos which can be included on your website.

Inserting an image

Thomas Tripp wants to include the Travelbug logo on his newly designed website. To do this he selects **Insert, Picture** from the **File** menu (Figure 141). The **Set Transparent Color** option from the *Picture* toolbar will allow Thomas to remove the white background so that the logo blends nicely into the page.

Figure 141 The picture called 'logo' has been selected from the Travelbug folder, and a thumbnail is displayed

TiP

Do remember that large picture files can take a long time to download. It is best to size the graphic in the graphics program prior to exporting it to a web page, to reduce the file size.

You can edit a graphic in FrontPage – for example, to resize or crop it. However, the file size will not reduce if you choose this method. Also, you cannot add more pixels when enlarging a graphic in FrontPage, so the effect is to make the graphic appear jagged.

Skills check ▶▶

Positioning, cropping, resizing, grouping and borders are controlled in the same way as in Microsoft Word. See pages 100 and 102 for details.

Just as in other applications, FrontPage's *Picture* toolbar will allow you to make changes to a graphic, such as rotating it, adjusting the brightness or even creating an automatic *thumbnail*. Thumbnails are often used on web pages to decrease download times – the visitor to the website can decide which images to see in full size, usually by clicking on them.

Another useful feature of FrontPage is that you can create a *photo gallery* of pictures very quickly by using **Insert, Web Component** and then selecting **Photo Gallery**. You can choose from four different layouts. In each case, thumbnail images of your files are created automatically (Figure 142).

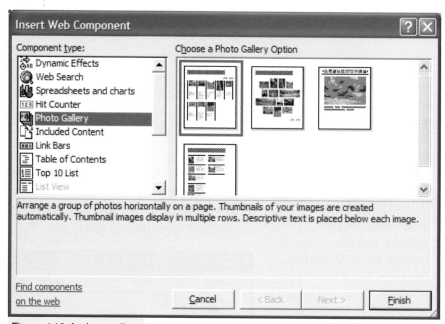

Figure 142 A photogallery

Skills check ▶▶

For information on choosing the most appropriate image resolution for print and screen, see page 147.

An advantage of producing a photogallery automatically with FrontPage is that the file sizes of the images are reduced substantially when the thumbnails are created. In the photogallery in Figure 143, each thumbnail is 4 KB, whereas the original images were all in excess of 1000 KB. Of course, if you keep the original images as part of your web (so that clicking on the thumbnail displays the full-size image) then the overall file size of your project will increase.

TiP

In order to look good when viewed on screen, images used on a website should contain about 72 pixels per inch. If you use too large a number of pixels, the image will take a long time to download.

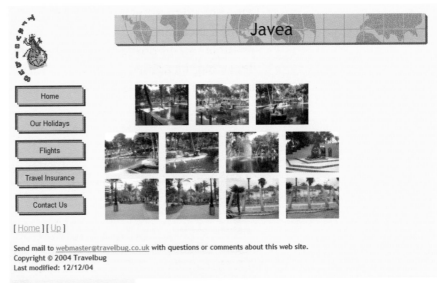

Figure 143 Thumbnails

Wrapping text

You can change the properties of an image to control how text wraps around it.

Figure 144 Changing how text wraps around an image

Double-click the image to display its *Picture Properties* dialogue. Click on the *Appearance* tab and make your selection for the **Alignment**, as shown in Figure 144.

Adding lines and simple shapes

You can add lines and shapes, fill the shapes with colour, outline them and make them look three-dimensional. The method in FrontPage is the same as in PowerPoint and the other Microsoft Office tools.

The **Autoshapes** button on the *Drawing* toolbar can be used to add shapes, including lines, a flow chart, stars, banners and callouts. It is possible to add borders to text and objects, as shown in Figure 145: Travelbug have used a *callout* on their Contact Us page, and have used a border around the text on their Insurance page.

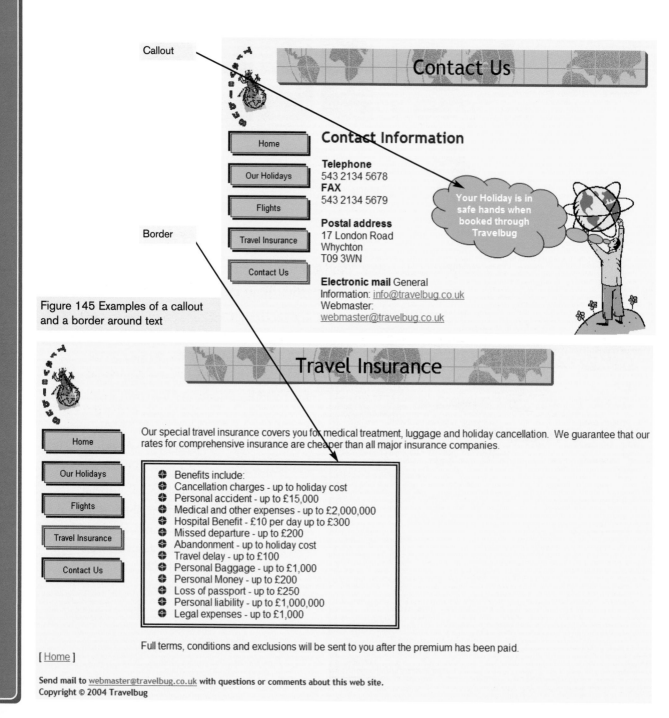

Figure 145 Examples of a callout and a border around text

Inserting hyperlinks

Click here to
add a ScreenTip

Figure 146 Adding a hyperlink and a ScreenTip

FrontPage will allow you to add *hyperlinks*, which allow visitors to the website to move from one page to another easily. Hyperlinks can also be used to move to different parts of a page or even to a different website.

You have the option of using text, buttons or pictures as hyperlinks. For example, on the Cruise Club web page, Thomas Tripp has created a hyperlink to the online application form (Figure 146). He has done this by typing the text, selecting it and then choosing **Insert, Hyperlink** from the menu.

✓ **TiP**

*It is helpful to add a **ScreenTip** which pops up when the user points at the hyperlink with their mouse. Figure 146 shows the button that allows you to add this feature.*

Furthermore, when you are creating a set of web pages (a 'web') using certain wizards, FrontPage automatically creates a *navigation bar* that has hyperlinks to the other pages in the web. These hyperlinks allow the visitor to move to a different page when the appropriate link is clicked. In Figure 147 the main navigation bar shows user-friendly *button hyperlinks*, whereas the hyperlinks at the bottom of the web page are examples of *text hyperlinks*.

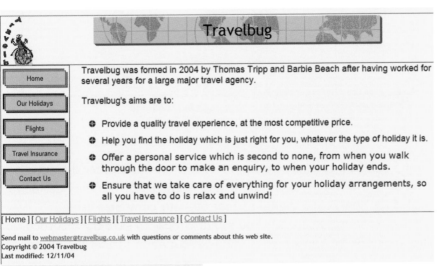

Figure 147 Hyperlinks on a web page

185

Including sounds

FrontPage allows you set a background sound for a web page. With your mouse, right-click on the page area while in Normal view and select **Page Properties** from the pop-up menu. The sound can be set to loop a set number of times, or to play the entire time the user is viewing a page.

Thomas Tripp of Travelbug decided to set the background sound of the company's Cruise Club page to the sound file 'Sailing', which he included in his PowerPoint presentation (see page 136). The *Page Properties* dialogue box he used is shown in Figure 148.

Figure 148 Adding a sound to a web page in FrontPage

Sound can be attached also to 'hover buttons' and other dynamic effects. If you have a microphone and sound card, you may decide to record the sound in a digital format on your computer using Microsoft Sound Recorder. You might choose to save the recorded sound as a WAV file, which is the most common format for sound files and the easiest for users to play, since all recent browsers can open WAV files.

TiP

WAV files can be very large. If you are going to put a WAV file on a web page, you can keep the size down by making it very short, or by using lower-quality recording settings. You could decide to compress the file into MP3 format.

TiP

It is important to keep an animated GIF's file size down. There is no compression between GIF frames, so you can end up with an extremely large file. Also, animated GIFs should be used sparingly, as any motion – particularly repetitive motion – can be very distracting for the user of the website.

Including animation (movement)

There are a number of ways in which you can include animation on your website.

Scrolling text

FrontPage allows you to add what it calls *marquees*. These are text areas that will *scroll* across the screen repeatedly. They are useful for getting a message across. Travelbug could include a marquee on its Cruise Club page: 'Don't delay … join now!'

Animated GIFs

You could include an animated GIF file, which consists of a series of static GIF images that are displayed in succession to create the illusion of movement. It is possible to download the Microsoft GIF Animator for free use in order to create animated GIF files for a website.

Dynamic HTML

You can use the *dynamic HTML* facility within FrontPage to animate text in a number of ways. For example, you could animate text to fly in from the right when a page is loaded, or you could format the text to change size when the mouse is moved over it. Figure 149 shows the *DHTML Effects* toolbar.

Figure 149 The dynamic HTML toolbar

Using transitions

As in PowerPoint presentations, you can apply transitions. FrontPage allows you to apply transitions to a web page for when a user enters or exits a page, or when the user enters or exits your website. You are

Skills check ▶▶

Setting page transitions for a PowerPoint presentation is explained on page 138.

able to choose the transition effect that you want, or choose random transition, so that the effect will change each time a user enters or leaves your website or web page (Figure 150).

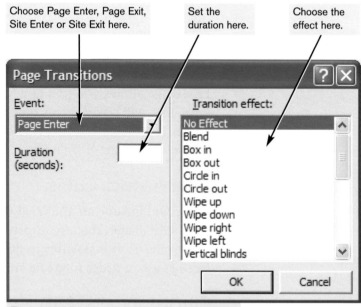

Choose Page Enter, Page Exit, Site Enter or Site Exit here.

Set the duration here.

Choose the effect here.

Figure 150 Dialogue box for page transitions

★ Assessment Hint

It is important to bear in mind the size limits for your e-portfolio. You may need to adjust the interactive components you include in view of this.

You can also set the time for the transition in seconds by entering a value in the *Duration (seconds)* text box.

Publishing the Web

In FrontPage, a 'web' does not become a website until it has been published and can be viewed by other people. A *web host* is the name given to the company that provides space on a web server for you to publish your site. Many companies will offer to publish websites free of charge on condition that they display some advertising banners at the top of each page. Alternatively, your school or college may have their own web server onto which you can publish your site.

Your own ISP may offer limited free space to publish your site. If you wish to publish your 'web' as it has been created in FrontPage, you need to find out whether your ISP supports FrontPage Server Extensions.

The steps necessary to upload the files that make up your website can vary from one ISP to another, but it is normally quite a simple process.

Project planning software

When you read through the section on project planning (page 199), you will see how important it is to prioritise tasks and to allocate time for each task, while at the same time ensuring you complete everything in the time available. In that chapter we suggest you produce a *mind map* and a *Gantt chart* to help you plan your project. Project planning software is available to help you do this.

You need to learn about

✓ how to create and modify mind maps

✓ how to create and modify project plans.

Mind mapping software

A mind map is a useful way to organise your ideas in the early stages of a project. See page 205 of the Project Planning section for more information about mind mapping.

Although it is easy to create mind maps on paper (for example, using a flip chart), remember that you may want to modify your mind map over time. Various software packages are available to help you create and modify mind maps; specialist packages include Inspiration and MatchWare OpenMind, although general diagramming tools such as Microsoft Visio can also be used.

By using software to create your mind maps, you will find it easier to add them to your e-portfolio as evidence of the planning you have done for your project.

Go out and try!

An example of a hand drawn mind map for an 18th birthday party is illustrated on page 206. Figure 151 shows how the same mind map would appear when prepared using mind mapping software. Find out what software packages are available to you that would be suitable for creating and editing mind maps and prepare your own version.

Figure 151 A simple mind map diagram created in Microsoft Visio

Project planning software

Whilst you can produce a project plan by hand or by using standard packages, the advantage of using a specialist software package such as Microsoft Project is that you can very easily modify the plan to reflect any changes you have to make during the project.

To create a project plan, you simply enter the tasks you have to complete, prioritise them, and specify the duration of each task together with the start and finish dates. The software will produce a Gantt chart that shows exactly how the project should be managed.

You can even use the built-in calendar to indicate any days that you will not be able to work on the project (Figure 152). Then the tasks will be scheduled around this time.

If you experience a hold-up in the work which means you cannot keep to the original schedule, you can amend the data you entered into the software; a modified Gantt chart will be produced to help you manage your time.

Project planning software is used extensively by organisations that run large projects. Figures 153–155 show the software in use by a construction company that had a project to build an extension to a house. The client had been given a completion date and it was important that the construction company were off the site by this date.

During the project the plasterers were held up on another job and were several days late in starting. This meant that other trades were also held up and the project had to be rescheduled. The project planning software made this task much easier and helped to ensure that the project was completed on time.

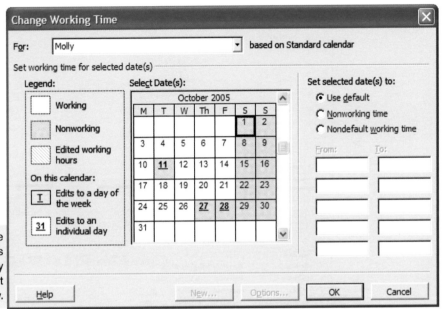

Figure 152 Molly will not be working at the weekends and has three days of holiday booked. Any plans will take this into account automaticallly.

	ⓘ	Task Name	Duration	Start	Finish	Predecessors
1		Set site up	1 day?	Mon 11/10/04	Mon 11/10/04	
2	▦	Foundations	2 days	Mon 11/10/04	Tue 12/10/04	
3		Drainage	1 day?	Wed 13/10/04	Wed 13/10/04	2
4		Sub structure brickwork	2 days	Thu 14/10/04	Fri 15/10/04	3
5	▦	Oversite and slab	1 day?	Fri 15/10/04	Fri 15/10/04	
6		Brick/blockwork	5 days	Mon 18/10/04	Fri 22/10/04	5
7		Timber roof structure	3 days	Mon 25/10/04	Wed 27/10/04	6
8	▦	Roof covering	4 days	Mon 01/11/04	Thu 04/11/04	
9		Velux installation	1 day?	Thu 28/10/04	Thu 28/10/04	7
10	▦	Soffits and facias	3 days	Tue 02/11/04	Thu 04/11/04	
11		Windows	1 day?	Fri 05/11/04	Fri 05/11/04	10
12		Knock through	3 days	Mon 08/11/04	Wed 10/11/04	11
13	▦	Plumbing 1st fix	2 days	Tue 09/11/04	Wed 10/11/04	
14	▦	Electrical 1st fix	2 days	Wed 10/11/04	Thu 11/11/04	
15	▦	Plastering	4 days	Mon 15/11/04	Thu 18/11/04	
16		Screeding	1 day?	Fri 19/11/04	Fri 19/11/04	15
17	▦	Tiling	4 days	Mon 29/11/04	Thu 02/12/04	
18	▦	Plumbing 2nd fix	2 days	Thu 02/12/04	Fri 03/12/04	
19	▦	Electrical 2nd fix	2 days	Thu 02/12/04	Fri 03/12/04	
20		Decorating	5 days	Mon 06/12/04	Fri 10/12/04	19
21		Hoist	1 day?	Fri 03/12/04	Fri 03/12/04	17
22	▦	Move bath	2 days	Thu 02/12/04	Fri 03/12/04	

Figure 153 Details of the building project are recorded in the software

Figure 154 A Gantt chart is automatically produced

Figure 155 The final stages of the project were rescheduled to take account of the delay in plastering. The grey rectangles show the original baseline and the blue rectangles show the new schedule.

Go out and try!

1 Referring to the mind map you created earlier, use project planning software to create a list of the tasks that need to be done for you to produce the yearbook.

2 Go through each task and give it a duration, and set up any dependencies between tasks (for example, you can't print the yearbook before it has been written and proofread).

3 A Gantt chart should be automatically produced. Edit this if necessary (for example, you might find that two things must be done in parallel if the yearbook is to be finished by the end of term).

Open your 'Project planning software' file. Create a new bold heading called '**Project planning software**' and describe the skills you have demonstrated in this activity.

Collaborative software

The summative project for Unit 4 will be a team effort, which you will develop with a group of other students in your school or college. For the duration of the project, you will work together to define the objectives, review progress and make decisions that will determine the final outcome. You will be working as a member of a team in a similar way to thousands of people in industry and commerce who carry out their day-to-day work as members of project teams.

Project teams use special software, known as *collaborative software* or *groupware*, to manage their work. Collaborative software enables groups of people working together to communicate effectively, to share documents, and to monitor and update the progress of a project. If your school or college hosts a virtual learning environment (VLE), such as Moodle, you may already be familiar with collaborative software.

> ✔ **TiP**
>
> *There are many software packages available to support collaborative working. These include **DiDAFolio, Digital Brain, Macromedia Breeze, Microsoft MSN** and **Moodle.***

LEARNING OUTCOMES

You need to learn about
✓ **using software to work as a team.**

However, you do not have to use sophisticated software to work together successfully in a team. Providing you have access to a network, intranet or the Internet, there are many features built into standard software applications that can help you.

- Microsoft Outlook offers options to send email attachments as 'shared documents' and to share calendars.

- You can save a document as 'read-only' so that people can view the document but cannot make changes.

- Password protection ensures that documents remain confidential, since users without the password will be unable to open the file.

- You can use templates to ensure that all team members adopt a consistent approach when creating documents and presentations.

- You can use the reviewing tools to show proposed changes to a document.

- Document reviewers can add comments, which the rest of the team can view.

○ A document library enables team members to share a collection of files, which can be viewed through a web browser or network. Users are notified by email whenever a team member adds or changes a file, and it is easy to see whether documents are draft or final versions.

Communicating with members of a team

The telephone and email are probably the most widely used methods of communication today. However, telephone calls are usually just between two people, which means that most members of the group cannot take part in the conversation. An email, on the other hand, can be sent to any number of people so that all group members receive the same information. Features such as the ability to create mailing groups, forward messages and attach files make email an ideal method of communication for members of a team. Refer again to the Email skills chapter (page 160) to remind yourself just what email does offer.

Sharing files with other members of a team

Whilst email is usually a successful way of sharing files, some email systems will not accept attachments over a certain size, or may not accept attachments at all. Occasionally files can accidentally be forwarded to the wrong people; this could pose a security problem.

Collaborative software enables users to share files of any size and type. The files can be viewed or edited by multiple users anywhere in the world at the same time. One advantage of this is that there will only be one version of the file in use, so all members of the team have access to up-to-date and reliable information. You can set up a document library that will enable team members to share files.

If project management files, such as a Gantt chart, are available for all team members to view, this will help to ensure that everybody is working to an up-to-date project timescale.

Creating and using shared folders

How much time do you spend looking for data files because you haven't organised your folders clearly? Imagine the possible delays to a group project if the team couldn't find their files quickly! To make sure that project files and documents can be accessed quickly and stored consistently by all team members, it is essential that a suitable folder hierarchy is created from the outset of any project and that team members adopt a consistent approach when naming documents.

It can be useful to share folders with other people on the same computer (who log in with different accounts) or with other people on the same network. To do this, right-click the folder you wish to share, and select **Properties** from the menu that appears. You can use the *Sharing* tab (see Figure 156) to make the folder available to other people.

? Think it over ...

Why might using a collaborative software application be safer then using shared folders? (Hint: think about deleting files.)

Figure 156 Sharing a folder across the network

Working collaboratively on a document

Whilst working on your project, it is highly likely that several team members will need to work on the same document. For example, it may be that individual team members each initially create part of a document, and the final work is assembled from the separate parts. Or perhaps individual team members are each researching different costs which must be incorporated in a large overall spreadsheet. By sharing documents, all team members can look at and work on the most up-to-date version of each.

You may choose to nominate just one member of your project team to make the final edits to a document. Before the document is finalised, it is possible for all team members to view the proposed changes and make their comments. The particular features of standard application software that enable you to do this are accessed through **Tools, Track Changes** and **Insert, Comment**.

Original

The first project meeting will be held on Wednesday 1 February 2006. I suggest we meet at 11.30 in Room E21. It will give provide an opportunity to discuss general project ideas.

Changed version with Track Changes

The first project meeting will be held on Thursday 2 February 2006. I suggest we meet at 09.00 in Room E21 with a second meeting at 14.00 which will provide an opportunity to discuss general project ideas.

| Deleted: Wednesday |
| Deleted: 1 |
| Deleted: 11.30 |
| Deleted: . It |
| Deleted: give |

Comment [PDS1]: Megan – I can't make 14.00. Peter.

Final version with changes accepted

The first project meeting will be held on Thursday 2 February 2006. I suggest we meet at 09.00 in Room E21 with a second meeting at 14.00 which will provide an opportunity to discuss general project ideas.

Figure 157 You can see how changes to the original text have been tracked. The deleted text is shown in the margin and added words appear in red. A comment has been added by one of the team.

Setting up a collaborative working environment

If you have a group of people working on the same project, one of the most important requirements is that all team members are using the same version of the software. In some software applications, changes made in the most recent version are not effective in older versions.

It may also be necessary to set up permission levels that specify whether team members are allowed to edit documents or merely to read them. It may be necessary to ensure that some documents can be viewed by only certain team members. Confidential documents may require password protection.

Maintaining a team diary

The ability to set up group meetings knowing that everybody in the team is available can save a lot of time and frustration. A common diary framework, often found in collaborative software, can detect when meeting times will work for everyone and send automatic reminders beforehand to ensure that nobody forgets to attend. With large and scattered project teams, a diary can also help you to track someone down: all their day-to-day appointments will be recorded.

Microsoft Outlook has a calendar feature that can be shared with team members over a network, intranet or even the Internet.

Figure 158 The calendar in Microsoft Outlook. Notice the option to open a Shared Calendar

All projects have a number of common characteristics:

- clear objectives
- a definitive outcome
- a fixed period of running time
- the possibility of being broken down into a sequence of smaller tasks.

LEARNING OUTCOMES

You need to learn about

✓ the questions you should ask yourself about your project brief

✓ how the success of your project will be judged

✓ how to create a project plan.

Most things you do, no matter how simple or complex, require careful planning and preparation in order to be successful.

Before you start it is essential to

- read the whole project brief carefully
- decide/understand what you have to do
- create appropriate directory/folder structures to organise your e-portfolio.

Even something as straightforward as baking a birthday cake needs planning to ensure you have the exact ingredients, the right size of baking tin and sufficient time for it to bake in the oven.

An example

Organising a holiday requires careful planning. Frankie and Sam would like to go on holiday together. Before they visit Travelbug to make their booking they must have a clear idea of where they would like to go, what they would like to do, and how much time they can afford to spend away from home.

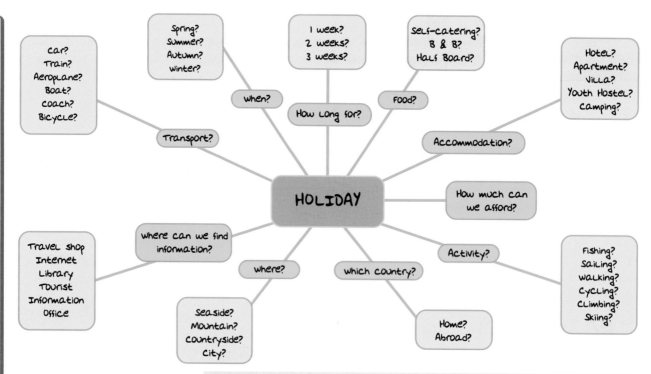

Figure 159 Frankie and Sam's spider diagram records all their suggestions and ideas

They both have so many suggestions and ideas that they decide to write them all down to be sure everything will be taken into consideration before reaching a final decision (Figure 159).

After much discussion they agree on a two-week camping and sports activity holiday in the French Alps. Now that they have a clear goal, they can really begin the preparations for their holiday. These preparations will include

- researching the holiday market and booking the holiday
- obtaining passports
- arranging travel insurance and medical insurance
- preparing for the sports activities – perhaps by getting fit and buying suitable clothing and footwear
- buying foreign currency
- arranging for their pets to be cared for
- arranging transport to the station or airport.

By the time they leave, Frankie and Sam will have put considerable effort into the planning and preparation of their holiday, so it should be a great success.

The same is true for the projects you will be completing in order to achieve your Certificate or Diploma in Digital Applications: if the projects are not planned carefully they are unlikely to be successful!

Your project brief

Assessment Hint

You will be provided with a detailed summative project brief (SPB) for both of the modules that comprise the Certificate in Digital Applications, or the modules that comprise the Diploma in Digital Applications.

Jargon buster

Objectives are the practical tasks that will enable you to achieve the overall aim of the project. Good objectives are said to be **SMART**:

Specific
Measurable
Agreed
Realistic
Time-constrained.

In other words, you should make sure that the tasks you set are achievable in terms of your own skills, the resources that are available to you and the time you have to complete them. Keep this in mind when you start to plan your project in more detail.

A well-written brief will enable you to identify the key features of the project. Spend time reading the project brief to familiarise yourself with its contents. After studying it, you should be able to provide answers to the following questions, which will eventually form the basis of your overall plan.

What have I been asked to do?

The answer to this question will reveal the overall purpose of the project. This may be to

- carry out research on a particular topic and present your findings
- create multimedia products
- produce images and artwork
- explore and plan for a business activity.

What do I have to produce?

When you are clear about the overall aim of the project, you should study the project brief more closely and make a list of all the separate items you must produce. These may be a combination of text, graphics, images or sound. For example, you may have to produce a letter, a web site, a presentation, a graphic image, a leaflet and a report. The items in your list will become the *objectives* of the project.

Why am I doing it?

Once you have established what you have been asked to do and what you are going to produce, you should think about *why* you are doing the work. This will ensure that your 'products' are entirely suitable for their purpose.

There will usually be a specific reason for producing the product:

- writing a report to convince people that something should change or remain the same

- producing a series of publications to educate people about a topical issue
- producing a multimedia product to convey a message to the public
- producing a graphic image to promote a product or event.

If you are unclear in your own mind as to the reason you are doing the work, it is highly likely that your audience will also have difficulties in understanding your message. To be successful you must make sure that your products convey the message in the most appropriate way.

Who are the target audience?

Another important point to consider is what type of people your product is directed at. In other words, who are the *target audience*? You would be expected to choose different methods for conveying the same information to children compared with adults.

For example, a poster aimed at children should be quite simple and straightforward, whereas you might use a more subtle approach for adults. If you were producing a written report for technical experts it would be quite acceptable to use technical language. However, you would have to reduce the level of technical jargon if the same report were to be presented to members of the general public.

It is important that you choose an appropriate style for your audience whilst ensuring that your finished product is also fit for its intended purpose.

TiP

Make sure you allocate some time to dealing with the unexpected. It is very unusual for everything to go smoothly, so there will almost certainly be unforeseen problems and delays along the way.

When do I have to have it finished?

Think about your timescale and how you will fit everything in. You should expect to spend a total of about 30 hours on each project. Take into account the time you will spend on planning and preparation in addition to actually producing your products.

Include time to review your work, and allow other people time to test your products. You will almost certainly need to modify or amend your work, and this must *all* be completed within the time allocated for the project.

TiP

If you wish to use a photograph that somebody else has taken, you must remember the law relating to copyright and obtain written permission to use the image. This will also take time.

Allow time to locate and order multimedia components, such as video and audio recordings from film libraries or video collections, if you need to include these in your project.

TiP

If a resource is going to be difficult to access, it might be worthwhile considering if there is an alternative way of achieving the same outcome.

Assessment Hint

You must ensure that your work complies with the technical specification outlined in the summative project brief. Make sure you follow the guidance given about file formats, download times and the overall size of the e-portfolio.

It is important that you do not take on something too ambitious that you will not be able to finish properly because you run out of time!

What resources can I use?

Each of the summative project briefs will include links to relevant websites or titles of textbooks that may help you. You will clearly have to use other resources too.

Some resources – such as school or college library books, the Internet, computers and printers – are probably readily available to you, but others may not be. For example, you may need to use specialist software or equipment that is available only at school or college, and you might need to share it with 20 or 30 other students. Alternatively, you might need to obtain books or other media from an outside source such as a library. This can take time to arrange.

If you know that something is going to be difficult to get hold of or restricted in use, you must keep this uppermost in your mind when planning your project. Furthermore, you must remember to record details of the sources of all the materials you use and to include these as evidence in your e-portfolio.

What else do I need to consider?

If you are working on artwork and images, you will also need to consider how the image is to be published. Consider, for example, whether it is to be published on screen or printed on paper. You can clearly see how an image will be viewed as part of a screen-based publication, but it is more difficult to visualise an image incorporated in a paper-based document. Carefully check the size of the image, the position on the page, and so on.

How will the success of your project be judged?

Your work will be presented in an e-portfolio that will be reviewed by your assessor and the moderator from the examining body, Edexcel. You will not be there to show them where to find the evidence of your work, so *your e-portfolio must be well structured and easy to use.* Follow the advice on creating e-portfolios given in the summative project briefs and in Skills section 5 (page 218).

You will be assessed against a number of activities, including
- planning and managing your project
- reviewing your project
- presenting evidence in an e-portfolio.

The other activities differ for each project, and more information is given in the appropriate chapters. Each activity carries a range of marks, and the marks are awarded according to the complexity of each activity.

The questions the assessor or moderator will have in mind when assessing your work are

- Is the product fit for the purpose?
- Is the product fit for the intended audience?

The safest way to make sure the assessor or moderator can answer 'Yes' to these questions is to make certain your work is reviewed throughout production and that you take notice of any points your reviewers make.

Who will review my work, and when?

It is very easy to get sidetracked and to lose sight of the original objective when you are working under pressure. A fresh pair of eyes can sometimes help to show where you have gone adrift. So for this reason you must make sure that you ask someone to look at your work at regular intervals to ensure it is fit for both the purpose and the intended audience.

You could ask your teacher, or maybe your friends or a member of your family, to help you. You could find someone who falls into the target audience category and ask him or her for an opinion.

You should show your product to a variety of different people and welcome their opinions. Constructive feedback is very valuable and is not a criticism of your work but is offered to help you improve your work and thereby achieve better marks. Listen to what other people say and consider their ideas carefully. You may not always agree, but a second opinion is always worth thinking about.

TiP

Remember that when you start to plan your project in detail you must ensure you allow time for other people to look at your work during production as well as at the end.

Getting started

When you have read through the summative project brief, ask your teacher or tutor to explain anything you do not understand. In this way you will avoid wasting valuable time by starting work on something that is not required!

You might find it helpful to produce a table, similar to the one in Figure 160, where you can make notes as you work through the project brief. It will help to ensure that nothing important is overlooked. It will also form the basis for the detailed project planning that must be done before you start work.

What have I been asked to do? This is the overall aim.		
What do I have to produce? These are the objectives.	Why am I doing it? This will help you focus on the purpose.	Who are the target audience?
1	1	1
2	2	2
3	3	3
4	4	4
5	5	5
6	6	6
7	7	7
8	8	8
9	9	9
10	10	10
When do I have to have the project finished?		
What resources can I use?		
Who will review my work?		

Figure 160 A chart to help you organise your thoughts

Project ideas

You are now almost ready to embark on your project, but you are still not ready to switch the computer on! There are a few more issues to be considered.

First you need to come up with some ideas. One of the most successful ways of doing this is to hold a brainstorming session with a group of friends – just like Frankie and Sam when they were planning their holiday! Record everything you can think of so that nothing is forgotten or overlooked.

Some people find a simple hand-written list is a good method of keeping track of ideas. One of the most popular methods is to produce a *mind map*. Mind maps help you organise your thoughts on one page so that you can see the relationship between one idea and another, and your ideas can flow from one topic to the next. Simple images can help you focus your ideas in a fun way.

Record the main topic at the centre of the page. From there, branch out and add the major themes around the main topic. Add associated ideas with further branches. Once your mind map is finished you can weigh up the pros and cons of the various ideas before coming to a decision.

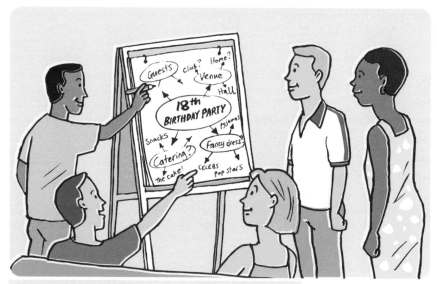

Figure 161 Mind map for planning an 18th birthday party

This mind map (Figure 161) was used to help plan an 18th birthday party.

Be SMART (see page 201) and don't get carried away by grand ideas that go off at a tangent. Always keep the target audience and project objective in mind. Some good advice is to keep things relatively simple – think 'quality' rather than 'quantity'!

Your project plan

Jargon buster

A **milestone** is a checkpoint in a project, usually associated with the delivery of some version of a product. Your final deadline is a milestone, as are each of the points at which you intend to get your product reviewed.

After preparing a list of objectives from the summative project brief, your next job must be to rearrange the list into a logical sequence, remembering that some tasks may have to be finished before others can be started.

List the key milestones in each project, and, where possible, try to finish one thing before getting too involved in the next. Number the tasks in the order you will complete them.

Now look at each task in turn and break it down into a sequence of smaller tasks so that you know exactly what has to be done. Give each of the smaller tasks a number. Remember to include time to ask your reviewers to give you feedback on your work.

For example, if the first task is to conduct a survey amongst top-year students at your school or college, you might come up with a list like this:

1 Conduct a survey
  1.1 Prepare the questionnaire for the survey
  1.2 Test the questionnaire with three students
  1.3 Modify the questionnaire as necessary
  1.4 Distribute the questionnaire
  1.5 Record the results
  1.6 Analyse the results in a spreadsheet
  1.7 Prepare suitable graphs

Decide how much time to allocate to each part of the project and write down when you plan to start and finish each task. Remember that you should also include time to deal with anything that might go wrong.

You should repeat this process for each of the objectives you have identified. The flow chart in Figure 162 can be used to remind yourself of the steps to take when planning each project.

When you have planned your project in detail you must record the information in your project planning software.

Make sure you include details of the tasks and sub-tasks. These should be in the order in which you will carry them out, and should show how much time you will spend on

Rearrange tasks into a logical sequence

Number each task

Break each task down into smaller tasks or stages and number each of these stages

Consider the resources you will need

Allow time for your work to be reviewed whilst in production

Allow time for your work to be modified as a result of the review process

Allow time for contingencies or unforeseen delays

Decide when you will start and finish each task

Figure 162 Planning a project

each and when you will ask your reviewers for feedback. You should also include

- task descriptions
- start dates
- finish dates
- times allowed
- notes to record progress and changes made to the plan.

Ask your teacher or tutor to approve your plan before you start any work on the project. As you complete each task, update your project plan. Keep a record of any changes you had to make to the plan, and say why.

Use the plan to help you meet your deadlines and finish your project on time. Every time you need to modify your plan you must save it with a new filename so that you can provide evidence of the development of your project from the beginning to the end. Don't be tempted to produce the plan after you have finished your project! Keep in mind that your teachers and the moderators who will look at the plan in your e-portfolio are very experienced and can usually discover the shortcomings!

Hints and tips

Assessment Hint

Don't forget to include in your e-portfolio demonstrations of how you used different software tools in your project. Screen captures can be useful for this.

Before embarking on your project work, you will have studied the skills chapters on word processing, spreadsheets, databases and so on. It is important that you make full use of these skills in order to create documents and on-screen publications that convey the message in the most effective way possible.

Here are some other hints to help you along the way:

- Remember to plan your e-portfolio before you start. Decide on the filenames you will use and make sure you know the appropriate format for publication in your e-portfolio. The summative project brief will specify the acceptable formats for each project. Don't waste time as you go along by converting every file into the final published format. It is a good idea to convert only the files that you will be presenting in your e-portfolio. You are less likely to get in a muddle if you do not have too many different versions of each file!
- Don't waste time in class working on things that can be done away from the classroom. Use the time you have with your teacher or tutor to get any help you need.

TiP

As you are doing an IT course, there is no excuse for presenting work that is inaccurate or poorly presented. If you have worked through the skills chapters in this book you should have picked up a lot of useful tips that will help you produce successful paper-based or screen-based publications.

○ Use folders and sub-folders to organise all your project work. Don't forget that you will be required to include evidence of your product from design through to implementation.

○ Save updates of your work regularly with different filenames. In this way, in the unlikely event you find yourself with a corrupt file, you can revert to the previous version and you will not have too much work to repeat. This will also help you demonstrate progress in your e-portfolio.

○ A USB memory stick is a good way of transferring your work between school or college and home. You will soon find the data files are too large to fit on to a floppy disk. Remember to scan your files for viruses!

○ Make regular backup copies of all your data files on CD as a safety precaution. Keep the backup copies in a safe place. It is sensible to save your project work on the school or college computer system as well as at home.

When you are happy that you can put a tick against each of the following points, then you have probably done as much as you can to ensure success:

○ Have you followed your plan and used it to monitor your progress?

○ Have you recorded and justified any amendments you made to the plan?

○ Can the history of the project be clearly seen from your plan?

○ Have you kept a record of *all* the resources you used?

○ Have you produced everything that you were asked to produce?

○ Does your document or presentation have an appropriate layout and structure?

○ Is the presentation style (font style, heading style, background colour, slide layout, and so on) consistent throughout?

○ Have you used page breaks sensibly?

○ Have you made effective use of space?

○ Have you chosen an appropriate font size?

○ Is it written in an appropriate language style to suit the target audience?

○ Have you spellchecked *and* proofread your work?

○ Have you used WordArt, clip art and colour in moderation?

○ Are the content and images relevant and suitable for the intended audience?

- Are your images clear and a sensible size?
- Are download times acceptable for images in your web pages?
- Does your document or presentation look professional?
- Have you reviewed your work and asked somebody else to test your product?
- Have you listened to their comments and modified your product if necessary? Remember to include evidence of your modified work in your e-portfolio.
- Is the product fit for the intended purpose?
- Do all navigation routes work?
- Have you saved your work in the specified file formats?
- Does the overall size of your e-portfolio comply with the technical specification?

Keep these guidelines in mind and you should be able to produce a first-class product that will meet all the original objectives.

Good luck with all your projects!

It is important that you undertake a thorough review of your project once it is completed. You should consider

- outcomes (the publications you have produced)
- process (how you worked)
- performance (the skills you have demonstrated).

You need to learn about

✓ collecting and presenting review evidence

✓ how to analyse the success of your project.

Introduction

Think back to Frankie and Sam and their two-week camping and sports activity holiday in the French Alps (page 199). Did you imagine that when they returned from their holiday they would forget all about it? Of course not! When they came home they would have discussed every aspect of the holiday. It is quite natural to look back on the experience, reflect on the good parts and try to work out why other aspects did not go quite so well. If they decide to repeat the holiday again some time in the future they won't want to repeat the mistakes too – they will want to have an even better time.

This is exactly the same process that you will carry out when you have completed each project. The process of reviewing your work is equally as important as actually carrying out the work in the first place. A thorough and effective evaluation will consider the *outcomes* (what you produced), the *processes* (how you produced it) and *performance* (your own contribution). You will make your own judgements and will also seek the opinions and views of a variety of other people in order to provide a comprehensive evaluation with suggestions for improvement.

You will have asked several people to review your project whilst you were working on it and you should have acted on their advice. You must also ensure that your finished product is reviewed by yourself and others.

Review evidence and presentation

The evidence you collect to show that you and other people have reviewed your project should be included in your e-portfolio. It may be presented in a variety of different ways.

For example, you may have provided a questionnaire for people to complete, so you could present the results graphically, drawing your conclusions from their responses. You may have received written evaluations, which could be scanned and presented as on-screen documents. Perhaps you have spoken to several people and can include a recording of your interviews. You may decide to prepare your own written evaluation, summarising the feedback you have received from other people together with your own thoughts. You might also consider producing your evaluation as a multimedia presentation or a video or audio diary. Your evidence is likely to be a combination of two or more of these suggestions.

Most things we do show that we all have strengths and weaknesses. Sometimes things turn out well and sometimes they are not so good. For example, one day we bake a cake that turns out to be rather flat, slightly burnt and generally disappointing. We show the cake to someone who has more experience, and he or she suggests that we might have used the wrong type of flour or had the oven temperature too high. We try again and next time the cake is much better.

Perhaps it will be obvious to you that some things did not go as well as you had planned and you recognise that there are weaknesses. In this case you will usually be very receptive to suggestions for improving it. However, it is more difficult to accept criticism when you think everything is all right, but do listen to what your reviewers have to say and do not be afraid to acknowledge weaknesses and to act on their suggestions for improvement.

Three important words to keep in mind when you are evaluating your work are *explain*, *justify* and *improve*. Imagine you are looking at a poster you have produced to make people aware of a forthcoming meeting. On reflection, you feel the font size you used was too small and not easy to read. In your evaluation don't just say 'The font size was too small' – instead *explain*, *justify* and *improve*! You might say 'The font size was too small for the poster to be read from a distance, and as a result it was not an effective publication. I should have used a font size of at least 72 point so that people passing by were aware of the date, time and place of the meeting. In addition I could have made better use of white space to make the important points stand out.'

When you were first given the summative project brief, you studied it and found answers to a series of questions:

- **What** have I been asked to do?
- **What** do I have to produce?
- **Why** am I doing it?
- **Who** are the target audience?
- **When** do I have to have it finished?
- **What** resources can I use?
- **Who** will review my work, and when?

In your evaluation you should consider whether you achieved everything you set out to do. Do not just answer 'Yes' or 'No' in each case – *explain* and *justify* your answers. What went wrong and why did it go wrong? On the other hand, what did you consider to be particularly successful and why was it a success? Were you able to make use of knowledge and skills that you already had? Alternatively, what new skills did you have to learn?

Consider the resources you used:

- Were some especially helpful and others not so useful?
- Did you have any difficulty in finding useful material?
- Were you able to use specific hardware and software successfully?
- Did you choose the most appropriate hardware and software?

Remember to *explain* and *justify* any statements you make.

- EXPLAIN who 'tested' your product during its production stages, why you asked that particular person and what their comments were. As a result of this feedback, what did you do to IMPROVE your product. Remember your 'product' might be a document, an image, a multimedia presentation or an on-screen publication. JUSTIFY your reasons for modifying your product or not modifying it.

- EXPLAIN why you asked for feedback from the people who looked at your finished project. Provide evidence that they have looked at your project, that you have considered their feedback and say whether or not you agreed with their comments. JUSTIFY your reasons for reaching your conclusions.

- How would you make sure things didn't go wrong again? What could you do better next time? Think about what you could do to IMPROVE things!

Finally, consider what you have learnt from the whole experience? Was your time plan realistic? Which areas of the project took longer than anticipated and why? Were there aspects of your own skill-base that were weak? Why? How would you rectify the weakness?

A successful evaluation will consider the project from every aspect. In particular, your assessors will be looking to see that you have reviewed the outcomes, the processes and your own performance.

Outcomes

✓ To what extent have the project's objectives been met?

✓ How effective are the final products?

✓ Are they fit for purpose?

✓ How could they be improved?

✓ Does the mix of components enhance the message you are trying to convey?

✓ Is the information organised in an appropriate manner?

✓ How well do your multimedia products function?

✓ Do you think their structure and mix of components work?

✓ How easy are they to use?

✓ Are the file formats and image resolutions suitable?

✓ Does your artwork convey the intended message?

Process

✓ How well did you plan your work?

✓ Did you manage your time well?

✓ Did you meet the deadline?

✓ What, if anything, went wrong?

✓ Did you choose the right or best people to review your project?

✓ Would you arrange the project differently next time?

Performance

✓ What have you learned from working on this project?

✓ Did you have appropriate ICT skills?

✓ What additional training do you feel you need?

✓ How well did you communicate your ideas to others?

✓ How could you further improve your work?

✓ What have you learned about yourself whilst working on this project?

✓ Were you able to draw on knowledge or skills you have acquired in other subjects?

✓ Are you proud of your achievements?

Creating an e-portfolio

You will create an e-portfolio to present evidence of your achievements. The assessor and the moderator will use your e-portfolio to judge your work, so you must make sure that it is self-explanatory and easy to use.

LEARNING OUTCOMES

You need to learn about

✓ what to include in your e-portfolio

✓ how to structure your e-portfolio

✓ how to test your e-portfolio.

What is an e-portfolio?

For most students, the idea of presenting coursework in electronic form rather than on paper is something quite new and challenging.

An e-portfolio is a multimedia stage designed to present your work. In this instance, the assessor and moderator must be able to find evidence of your achievements easily.

This is an innovative and exciting way of showing what you are able to do. Your work can come alive with graphics, animations and sound. It is environmentally friendly, saving pages and pages of paper, as well as being a very convenient way of taking your work from place to place. Ultimately your e-portfolio will contain additional information about you, your education and career and, in the longer term, is likely to be looked at by a wide range of people.

Your teacher or tutor will provide you with more detailed information on the system you will be using. However, ideally, you should be able to access your work from any PC wherever you choose: at school or college or at home.

★ Assessment Hint

All the work you produce as evidence towards your Certificate or Diploma in Digital Applications will be presented for assessment and moderation in an e-portfolio. You will not be required to submit any documentation on paper.

You have already looked at a wide variety of websites and are familiar with the features that make them pleasing to look at, easy to use and effective. You have evaluated their impact and appropriateness for the intended audience and looked at the combination of text and graphics, download times, and so on. Your aim is to replicate the successful features so that the assessor and moderator can easily find their way around your work. When you study each of the summative project briefs, notice how buttons and links take you from one section of the project to another, and how they also direct you to pages of hints and tips and back again to the main sections. Each one has been designed to make it easy for you to find your way around. Similarly, your e-portfolio must clearly guide users through your work.

Organisation of your e-portfolio

TiP

You will find it much easier if you plan the development of an e-portfolio alongside the planning of each project. In this way it is unlikely that important elements will be overlooked.

You must keep in mind that the people who will look at your e-portfolio will not have you at their side to help them find the evidence they will be looking for. The user interface is therefore an important element of any e-portfolio: it is essential that your e-portfolio be well organised, and structured so that anyone can find their way around it efficiently and without difficulty.

The skills you developed in Presentation Software and Web Authoring Software are equally applicable to your e-portfolio. Developing a storyboard, structure and flow charts will help ensure that suitable links are in place to make the e-portfolio easy to navigate and user-friendly.

The overall appearance of the e-portfolio is equally as important as the content. You must make sure that it is pleasing for users to look at, as well as being easy to use. Include a variety of interactive components such as buttons, hotspots, and links.

Content of your e-portfolio

The content will reflect the tasks set in the summative project briefs, so each e-portfolio will therefore be different from another. The project brief will set out in detail what should be included, but the basic structure of each e-portfolio will be similar and will include the following

- home page
- contents page or menu
- the final work you have produced, which may include letters or reports, presentations, web pages, images, etc.
- evidence and explanations of the work you carried out, such as
  - project planning and monitoring
  - the development stages of your work – images, presentations, brochures, web pages, and so on – with comments justifying any modifications made
  - references to sources of documents or graphical components
  - evidence of data collection
  - supporting evidence of database structures or spreadsheets
  - evidence of market research or surveys
  - storyboards, structure charts and flow charts
  - review and evaluation of the project process and outcomes
  - feedback from your reviewers and suggestions for improvement
  - bibliography
  - copyright information, including acknowledgements and permissions where applicable.

Saving your work

It is quite likely that people viewing your e-portfolio may not have access to the same software that you used to produce your documents, images, presentations and so on. For this reason it is essential that you save the work in your e-portfolio in suitable formats as outlined in the summative project brief. For example, paper-based documents are most likely to be in PDF format, whereas screen presentations such as web pages will be HTML files. Images will normally be saved as JPEGs, and multimedia presentations converted to Flash SWF format.

Accessibility and testing

When your work is finished and your e-portfolio is complete you must make sure it works properly. Do not rely solely on checking it for yourself – you know the way around your work and will not be able to provide totally unbiased feedback. Let somebody else who is not familiar with the contents look at it.

As a result of this feedback, it might be necessary to modify your e-portfolio. The important thing to remember is that it must be user-friendly so that the assessor and moderator can use it without help.

In particular you should check that

- the content is complete and includes everything detailed in the summative project brief
- the e-portfolio is clearly presented, easy to use, attractive and effective
- every link goes where it should go with no dead-ends
- the e-portfolio can be displayed correctly in different browsers (e.g. Internet Explorer and Netscape)
- download speeds are acceptable
- other people can use the e-portfolio without help.

Authentication

Finally your teacher or tutor must provide authentication to confirm that the work is your own.

✔ TiP

Sometimes it is helpful to give the person testing your e-portfolio a list of questions and ask him or her to find the answers. That person will have to rely on the links, instructions and explanations you have set up in your e-portfolio.

Go out and try!

This is an opportunity for you to produce a small e-portfolio to display evidence of the various skills you have learnt. It will also enable you to learn how to save files in suitable file formats and to check download speeds for images.

When you worked through the other skills sections you saved separate files describing the skills you had been using. You included headings for each of the activities and wrote a short description of the skills you had learnt. Can you use the headings to provide a link to the examples described?

Task

1 Design an e-portfolio that contains a home page which will direct users to three of the skills pages, and from there to two of the files that illustrate the skills described. Make sure that some of the pages include graphic images so that you can test the download speeds of the images.

For example, the flow chart in Figure 166 would result in a home page with three distinct buttons to link to the word-processing, spreadsheet and presentation skills files. From there, links would be set up to show the worked examples of the first two activities in each.

Figure 166 Flow chart

Before you create the e-portfolio, think about the file formats you should use to ensure your work can be viewed on any computer, such as using .pdf files for text pages. Ask your teacher to check that you have not forgotten anything important.

2 Ask your friends to test this e-portfolio. Consider any suggestions they make for improvement and modify your structure if necessary.

3 In turn, look at what your friends have produced and compare ideas. Think about why some e-portfolios might appear more user-friendly than others. Do you think your e-portfolio is the best possible showcase in which to display your achievements? How might you improve on your ideas when you produce the e-portfolio for your first assessment? Write a list of the improvements you might make and say why you think they are necessary – if you don't do this now you will almost certainly forget the improvements by the time you do your assessment! Save the list so that you can refer to it later.

TiP

For practice purposes it is not necessary to include more than a basic selection of activities. The object of the exercise is to create something that is user-friendly, pleasing to the eye, easy for someone to use and viewable on any computer.

Index

Let the web do the work!

Why not visit our website and see what it can do for you?

Free online support materials

You can download free support materials for many of our IT products. We even offer a special e-alert service to notify you when new content is posted.

Lists of useful weblinks

Our site includes lists of other websites, which can save you hours of research time.

Online ordering – 24 hours a day

It's quick and simple to order your resources online, and you can do it anytime – day or night!

Find your consultant

The website helps you find your nearest Heinemann consultant, who will be able to discuss your needs and help you find the most cost-effective way to buy.

It's time to save time – visit our website now!

www.heinemann.co.uk/vocational

 01865 888068   01865 314029   orders@heinemann.co.uk   www.heinemann.co.uk